INDIAN CLASSICAL SWEETS

HISTORY, TRADITION AND RECIPES

DR ANSHUMALI PANDEY

"To all the humble Halwais and their faithful customers".

Contents

Preface *ix*

1. Indian Sweets 1
2. Classification Of Indian Sweets 4

Classical Sweets & Desserts Of India

3. Aaam - Ras 9
4. Ada 11
5. Anarsa 13
6. Aval Puttu 15
7. Awan Bangwi 17
8. Bal Mithai 19
9. Balushahi 21
10. Barfi 23
11. Basundi 25
12. Bebinca 27
13. Boorelu 29
14. Cham Cham 31
15. Chhannar Payesh 33
16. Chhena Gaja 35
17. Chhena Jhili 38
18. Chhena Murki 40
19. Chhena Poda 42
20. Chikki 44
21. Danadar 47
22. Dehrori 49
23. Dharwad Peda 51
24. Dhondas 53
25. Dodha Burfi 55
26. Doodhpak 57

Contents

27. Double Ka Meetha 59
28. Gajak 61
29. Gavvalu 63
30. Ghari 65
31. Ghevar 68
32. Gujiya 70
33. Gulab Jamun 73
34. Halbai 76
35. Halwa 78
36. Imarti 81
37. Jalebi 83
38. Kaju Katli 86
39. Kaju And Pista Roll 88
40. Kalakand 90
41. Kanchagola 92
42. Khaja 94
43. Khapse 97
44. Kheer 99
45. Kheer Sagar 101
46. Khubani Ka Meetha 103
47. Koat Pitha 105
48. Kozhukatta 107
49. Kulfi 109
50. Laddoo 111
51. Lapsi 114
52. Lassi 116
53. Madhurjan Thongba 118
54. Makhan Mishri 119

Contents

55. Malpua 120

56. Malai Paan 122

57. Mambazha Pradhaman 124

58. Mawa Bati 126

59. Mihindana 128

60. Mishti Doi 130

61. Modak 132

62. Mohan Thaal 134

63. Mysore Pak 136

64. Naankhatai 138

65. Nap Naang 140

66. Narkol Naru 142

67. Obbattu 144

68. Chapter 68 146

69. Panasa Thonalu 148

70. Parippu Payasam 150

71. Pateesa (son Papri) 152

72. Patishapta 154

73. Peda 156

74. Petha 158

75. Pitha 160

76. Pongal 162

77. Pootharekulu 164

78. Pukhlein 167

79. Rabri (rabdi) 169

80. Rasabali 171

81. Rasgulla 173

82. Ras Kadam 175

Contents

83. Ras Malai 177

84. Rotana 179

85. Sael Roti 181

86. Sandesh 183

87. Shahi Tukra 185

88. Shankarpali (shakkarpara) 187

89. Sheer Khurma 189

90. Shor Bhaja 191

91. Shrikhand 194

92. Shufta 196

93. Sithabhog 198

94. Singori 201

95. Sohan Halwa 202

96. Sutarfeni 204

97. Thekua 206

98. Unni Appam 208

99. Vellum Nombu Adai 210

100. Zarda 212

101. Summary 214

102. Glossary Of Indian Sweets And Desserts 216

Know Your Author 221

Author's Qr Code 223

PREFACE

Indian Classical Sweets: History, Tradition and Recipes

Everyone is well aware of a slogan *"muh mitha kijiye"* whenever any auspicious event occurs in India. People say this because sweets are a vital element of every joy and happiness celebrated in this country. Whether it is related to the birth of a child, buying a new car or getting married, sharing sweets is a tradition that will always remain on. It has become a sign of expressing love and gratitude towards those who are close to you. Apart from marriages which initialize from distribution of sweets and end with the same, festivals are also playing a big role in distribution of sweets. All the Indian festivals are incomplete without its essence. Sweets are prepared in Indian households not only for special feasts and occasions, but also for no reason.

No Indian wedding is complete without boxes of sweet. Firstly let's just clarify what sweet is. Indian sweets, simple yes, but this is then broken down further to hundreds of different types of sweets from ladoo, barfi, besan, gulab jamun, petha, halwa and so much more. The choice of flavours are endless but it is a must at a wedding and any celebratory event, a birthday, birth of a baby or even passing your examinations.

Dr Anshumali Pandey

I

Indian Sweets

Everyone is well aware of a slogan "muh mitha kijiye" whenever any auspicious event occurs in India. People say this because sweets are a vital element of every joy and happiness celebrated in this country. Whether it is related to the birth of a child, buying a new car or getting married, sharing sweets is a tradition that will always remain on. It has become a sign of expressing love and gratitude towards those who are close to you. Apart from marriages which initialize from distribution of sweets and end with the same, festivals are also playing a big role in distribution of sweets. All the Indian festivals are incomplete without its essence. Whether it is Diwali, Holi, Pongal, Thrissur pooram, Chhath, Baisakhi, Feast of Three Kings, Bihu, Onam, Id ul Zuha and Id ul Fitror the day of celebrating bond of brother and sister i.e. Rashabandhan,they act as an essential part for each one of them. They are prepared in Indian households not only for special feasts and occasions, but also for simple celebrations like birthdays, anniversaries etc.The people who live close to their relatives go at each other's place and share the packets of sweets during Diwali. No Indian wedding is complete without boxes of sweet.

What is Indian Sweet: Indian sweets, simple yes, but this is then broken down further to hundreds of different types of sweets from ladoo, barfi, besan, gulab jamun, petha, halwa and so much more. The choice of flavours are endless but it is a must at a wedding and any celebratory event, a birthday, birth of a baby or even passing your examinations.

So why are Indian sweets mandatory to have for a celebration? According to Hindus, all the ingredients in mithais; sugar, milk, and ghee are considered to be "sattvic" which means pure and can be eaten by everyone, even spiritual leaders and vegetarians. As they are pure ingredients, mithai is also offered to the gods and distributed to the devotees in temples. Mithai is used to break fasts or eaten during a fast bearing in mind that the term mithai has no religious significance. This old tradition has been kept alive for centuries and mithai will always be served at times of celebrations. Moreover sweets can also be referred to as a "happy food" as they swiftly lighten up the mood and make you feel better. Indian sweets are known as "Mithai". They rely heavily on sugar, milk and condensed milk and frying, however the bases of the sweets vary by region. They are more intense and sweeter than western sweets and desserts and quite a bit heavier since they're made mainly in Ghee which is clarified butter.

India not only has a rich cultural history, its association with sweets is also millennia old. Sugarcane has been grown in the Indian subcontinent for thousands of years, and the art of refining sugar was invented there 8000 years ago (6000 BCE) by the Indus Valley Civilization. The English word "sugar" comes from a Sanskrit word sharkara for the refined sugar, while the word "candy" comes from Sanskrit word khaanda for the unrefined sugar– one of the simplest raw forms of sweet. The oldest reference to Jalebi was made in the 13th century. Over its long history, cuisines of the Indian subcontinent developed a diverse array of sweets. Some claim there is no other region in the world where sweets are so varied, so numerous, or so invested with meaning as the Indian subcontinent.

Some of the common ingredients used in Indian sweets are different flours, milk, milk solids, fermented foods, root vegetables, raw and roasted seeds, seasonal fruits, fruit pastes and dry fruits. The method of preparation are also quite diverse using techniques like freezing for kulfi, frying for jalebi and Imarti, roasting for Mysore pak, baking for nan khatai and simple cooking for gajar ka halwa among others. India is the largest consumer of sugar in the world at 26 million tonnes per year. The largest population in the world, China consumes far less at 16 million tonnes per year. Thus the love of Indians for sweets can be gauged from these figures. The taste and preferences of the populace have seen mercurial changes in the last few decades. Lately a keen interest has once again arisen in the traditional sweets in India, and to cater to the demands of the new generation. Indian Sweets like Pedhas, Barfis, Gulab Jamuns, Rassogollas, Jalebi, Halwa and a host of other sweets are in great demand today not only in India but also in foreign countries.

Earlier the facility of online shopping was not available so it was a bit difficult to gift these sweets to your loved ones who live quite far away from you. But now you have a large variety of sweets which can be ordered online and will be safely delivered to the place you want. Some of the famous sweets of India are–Bengali rasgullas, Kaju katli, petha etc. Apart from these traditional sweets, nowadays cakes and cookies are also very much in trend during these festivals. You can order these sweets online and can choose the type of packing that you like. They also provide a facility of low sugar sweets for the health conscious people or the one suffering from diabetes.

All sweets are available in various shapes and colours too. The one you will opt will be delivered without any fuss. You do not have to worry about the freshness and hygiene of these sweets because they assure you a pretty good quality. According to different seasons of festival, they provide the discount coupons as well and other offers such as one on one free. You can also get free gift covers during Diwali season on buying of a specific quantity of sweets and can also order different cakes as well according to the flavours you like. They provide different categories according to price and material used in sweets. Different toppings can be chosen if you like to add some extra tinch of taste in the sweets.

No matter if you are celebrating a little joy, festival or whatever, do not forget to share your happiness with others by giving them sweets in present because festivals are the perfect time to share your feelings and removing all the grudges between you and your beloved ones not just by words but sweets too. Moreover buying sweets is no more a big task; it's just one click away because of the online shopping facility available nowadays. They are available for the all age group people whether you are planning to gift them to kids in the form of chocolates or young ones in the form of traditional sweets because sweets are forever.

II

Classification of Indian Sweets

Though there are hundreds of Indian sweets they can broadly be divided into SIX categories:

1. Kheers and Payasams:

Kheers are like Puddings. It's rice pudding typically made by boiling rice with milk and sugar. It is often flavored with cardamoms, saffron, pistachios or almonds. While the dish is traditionally made with rice, it can also be made with other ingredients such as vermicelli (sewiyan) which is a thin noodle and also flour. Kheer is known as Payasam in the South of India. They tend to use coconut milk instead or regular milk.There are many versions of this dessert dish in both the south as well as North of India. It's an essential dish in many Hindu and Muslim feasts and celebrations. Payasams are served as an offering to the gods in South Indian Hindu temples during rituals and ceremonies. The Southern Indian state of Kerala, people have a particular affinity towards this dish.

2. Laddu/Laddoos:

Laddoos are like crumbly textured candy balls. They are usually made of flour and other ingredients formed into balls and sometimes dipped in sugar syrup. Like most other Indian sweets there are hundreds of variants of this ball of sweet goodness. Laddoos are very popular in India, and are an irreplaceable part of religious ceremonies. They are offered at temples for religious ceremonies, and later served as prasad (blessing from god) to people.The Motichoor Laddu or Boondi laddu is a popular type of laddoo found in India made from grilled gram flour flakes which are sweetened, mixed with almonds, pressed into balls and fried in ghee. The Besan (ground gram) ladoo is common in India. It is made from besan mixed with pieces of sugar. These laddoos are often finished by rolling them in nuts or dessicated coconut or syrup. Sometimes just a single nut or raisin is pressed into them.

3. Halvas:

Halva also spelled Halwa is a sort of cross between a pudding and candy. They are thick puddings made out of finely grated vegetables, milk, sugar and flavored with cardamom. They can also be grain based and made out of semolina or pulses like the mung bean. The semolina halwa known as Suji Halwa is common and popular in India. It is made with wheat semolina, sugar or honey, and butter or Ghee and topped with nuts and raisins. The halwa is very sweet with a gelatinous texture similar to polenta with the added butter giving it a rich mouthfeel. Gajar halwa or a halva made of carrots is also widely popular in India. It is prepared with condensed milk and ghee, without semolina to bind it together. The result has a moist yet flaky texture when freshly prepared.Some halvas are put in molds to give them a shape and neatly cut and garnished with a nut, raisin or beaten silver foil.

4. Barfis:

Barfi or Burfi is a sweet quite similar to fudge. Plain barfi is made from condensed milk, cooked with sugar until it solidifies. Plain barfi is made from condensed milk, cooked with sugar until it solidifies. Other varieties include besan barfi , made with besan (gram flour) and pista barfi , which is a milk barfi containing ground pistachio nuts. The name is derived from the Persian word _barf' which means ice since burfi is similar to ice in appearance. The bite sized Barfi is often flavoured with cashew, mango, pistachio and spices and garnished with a thin layer of edible silver leaf. There are hundreds of varieties of Burfi and can be shaped in a number of ways and cab be quite colorful. Some burfi is cut in to diamond shapes like the Kaju Katli (Cashew nut Burfi) while some are multi colored and rolled in to a sushi rice ball shape.

5. Kulfi:

While Ice cream is the probably the World's most popular dessert, India it's own frozen dessert called Kulfi.Kulfi is prepared from evaporated milk, sweetened condensed milk and heavy cream along with sugar. The mixture is boiled and thickened before it is cooled, put in molds and frozen. Unlike the Western ice creams, which are whipped and filled with air, kulfi is not whipped, which results in a solid and dense frozen dessert. Traditionally, kulfi is set in cone shape molds but can be frozen in any shaped molds or even ice trays.

6. Sugar Syrup Based Sweets:

Like the western doughnut which is dipped in a sugar syrup..many Indian sweets are deep fried and soaked in syrup as well. The syrup these sweets are often dipped into in India is usually aromatic and flavoured with saffron, rose water and cardamom. One of the most popular syrup based dessert is the Gulab Jamun. They are deep fried balls made of special dough and soaked in the aromatic sugar syrup. Another deep fried sugary delight is the Jelebi/Jalebi. The batter for Jalebis is piped directly in hot oil or ghee in circular shapes...a bit like a pretzel, then soaked in syrup. They're bright orange or yellow in colour and are very common around India and available at almost any sweet shop. It can be served warm or cold and has a somewhat chewy texture with a crystallized sugary exterior coating.

Classical Sweets & Desserts of India

(This Part contains most of the Important Sweet dishes of the Indian Subcontinent along with their Recipes).

III

Aaam - Ras

In Hindi, Aam means mango and Ras means Juice. So Aamras is basically Mango Juice or Pulp. It is also called Keri no Ras in Gujarati. This is a sweet which is considered as food made in heaven. Aamras or aam ras is a popular summer dessert or sweet from the western Indian states of Maharashtra, Uttar Pradesh and Gujarat. It is very popular both in Gujarat and Maharashtra. In fact, in both Gujarati and Maharashtrian weddingsaamras is an important part of the menu.Traditionally aamras is served with Poori and this combo of aamras puri is liked by many people and is quite popular. But aamras can also be had after a meal or as a sweet dish, dessert or just about at any time. It is made of sweet, juicy and ripe pureed mangoes flavored with sugar or jaggery. Mango is considered the king of fruits in India and no summer season is complete without the mention of aamras.A cup of Aamras makes a good energy booster, protects against dehydration in summers and has calming and antidepressant properties. Though its natural taste by itself is great, some people add more flavor to it by putting some rose syrup, saffron, dry ginger powder, cardamom or dry fruits like cashews, almonds etc.

Recipe:

Ingredients:

- Ripe alphonso mangoes – 4nos
- Sugar – 2 tbsp
- Cardamom powder – 1 tsp
- Saffron soaked in 4 tablespoons of milk – a pinch
- Slivered almonds and pistachios – for garnish

Method:

- Wash the mangoes and dip them in water for 2 – 3 hours.
- Now, with the help of fingers press the mangoes gently to loosen the pulp.
- Take off the tip and squeeze out the pulp in a clean bowl, discard the seed.
- Next, after squeezing them, peel it and extract the pulp completely. After this, if you find any pulpy lump, just take the whisker or wooden whisker (mathani) and whisk it well.
- Now add cardamom powder saffron milk, sugar and mix well.
- Garnish with slivered almonds and pistachios and serve with hot pooris

IV

Ada

Ada or Ela Ada, is an Indian sweet and traditional Kerala delicacy, consisting of rice parcels encased in a dough made of rice flour, with sweet fillings, steamed in banana leaf and served as an evening snack or as part of breakfast. It can be seen even in parts of Tamil Nadu as well. It is a snack made out of raw rice flour, sugar or jaggery and grated coconut. It is a heavenly yet healthy mixture, which has the sweetness of coconut and melted jaggery and sealed within a layer of steamed rice flour dough. Sometimes mashed bananas or ripe Jackfruit is also added. It is traditionally prepared in most parts in Kerala and enjoyed during festivals and occasions like on Onam and Vishu (the New Year of Keralites). It is also given as Prasadam (Sacred Food) to devotees at temples in Kerala. Ela means leaf, and this sweet rice pancake is named so because it gets a special aroma and flavour by being steamed in banana leaves. It makes for one of the healthiest delicacies out there since it is steamed and not fried in oil or ghee like most desserts.

Recipe:

Ingredients:

- Jaggery– 200 gms.
- Water to melt jaggery– 50ml For filling
- ghee – 2 Tsp
- Grated coconut – 1 cup
- Cardamom powder –½ tsp
- Hot water salted –60ml
- Rice flour – 1 cup

- Oil – 1 tsp
- Banana leaf to wrap (dipped in hot water to wrap)

Method:

- Pour some water in a pan and add the jaggery to it.
- Keep mixing gently to avoid the jaggery sticking to the surface of the pan, and melt the jaggery completely.
- In a wide sauce pan, roast a whole cup of freshly grated coconut in two tsps of ghee. Roast it for a few minutes until the colour of the coconut changes slightly.
- Once roasted, add the melted jaggery to the pan, pouring it through a sieve.
- Mix the coconut and jaggery together. Let it cook till it thickens.
- Add some cardamom powder and ghee now.
- Turn off the stove and let it cool.
- Pour some water in a pan and add some salt. Let the water come to a boil.
- Once the water starts boiling, turn off the stove.
- Take a cup of rice flour and a tsp of ghee in a mixing bowl.
- Pour the boiling water in the bowl and mix well.
- Mix the flour till you get nice tough dough.
- Now, take a banana leaf and cut it up into several pieces, to seal and cook the adas.
- Take some dough and roll it in your palm to form small balls.
- Flatten the dough and place it on the centre of the banana leaf piece. Pat the dough to flatten it evenly.
- Now, place some of the jaggery–coconut mixture in the centre and spread it.
- Fold the leaf and seal it, making sure to press down on all sides.
- Once the steamer is ready, place the banana leaf on the tray and put it in the steamer. Steam cook for about 10 to 15 minutes.
- Serve hot.

Tips: *You can increase or decrease the amount of jaggery used based on your taste preference. If you prefer your desserts to have less sweetness, you can decrease the quantity of jaggery to about 150 gms., and if you prefer it extremely sweet, then you can slightly increase the quantity.*

V

Anarsa

Anarsa is a type of sweet Marathi and Bihari dish made from rice flour, sesameseeds or poppy seeds, sugar or jaggery and desi ghee. Anarsas are made in two types- in the shape of round tablets or flat tablets. While eating round Ansara, it is crisp and soft from inside, which has a completely different taste. The term Anarsa or Anarasa may be originated from Anna means grains and Rasa means juiciness in Hindi dialect. (ann + ras = anarasa). It is important to note that Anarsa is considered pure compared to other sweets, so its demand is more in the festival. There is also a religious story related to this. If the scriptures are believed then it is believed that when Parvati offered prayers to get Lord Shankar, then she offered Lord Shankar in the form of prasadam. This is the reason why it is compulsorily used in Teej, the popular festival of Bihar, Uttar Pradesh and Jharkhand. The biggest feature of Anarsa is that it does not spoil quickly; it can be eaten comfortably for a week without keeping it in the fridge.

Adhirasam or Kajjaya in Kannada or Ariselu in Telugu a type Anarsa from Tamil Nadu cuisine. This is a sweet with a strong association with Diwali across homes in Tamil Nadu. The accompanying syrup known as the "paagu" is considered to be all important here. The consistency needs to be exactly right as depicted by the traditional adhirasam recipe. Usually made of flour, the adhirasam looks similar to a doughnut.

An old historical companion states that the adhirasam made an appearance in Tamil Nadu during the reign of the formidable Chola dynasty almost thousand years ago (1509–1529 C.E). There are inscriptions from the Vijayanagar Empire that suggest it was a popular sweet dish in Krishna Deva Raya's royal kitchen which was made from rice flour, jaggery, butter and pepper. It's not just a food of the royals but also a food of the gods, and is part of the temple offering (prasad) at many temples and also poojas at homes.

The yearly festival at the Panchavarnesvar Temple in Nallur, Tamil Nadu is characterized by an offering of adhirasam as it is considered to be a form of holy food during the celebrations. The sweet meat is prepared by following the traditional adhirasam recipe which is cooked within the temple premises itself between the hours of dawn to 11 PM in order to offer it to the deity at the stroke of midnight when the Pujas or the holy ritual begins.

Recipe:

Ingredients

- Rice flour – 1 cup (150 gms.)
- Jaggery– more than ½ cup (75 gms.)
- Sesame seeds – 3 to 4 tbsp
- Poppy seeds – 3 to 4 tbsp
- Ghee – for frying anarsa

Method:

- Finely crush the jaggery in mortar pestle.
- Take sesame seeds and poppy seeds in separate plate to coat the anarsa.
- Take rice flour in a big mixing bowl and add finely grind jaggery into it.
- Mix really well and knead smooth and firm dough. You'll need to mix jaggery in flour for around 6 to 7 minutes.
- Now cover the dough and keep aside for 15–20 minutes to set. Keeping the dough for over a day gives spongier anarsa.
- Heat enough ghee in a wok or pan to deep fry the anarsa.
- Dough is now ready, grease your hands with some ghee and pinch small size dough and roll giving it a round shape.
- Dust this dough ball with some sesame seeds and roll back again then flatten it slightly. You can also coat the anarsa with poppy seeds as well.
- Now gently slide the anarsa in medium hot ghee for deep frying and fry until golden brown and little crispy from both sides on low flame.

Drain out the fried anarsas on kitchen paper towels to remove excess ghee. Continue making the anarsa until the entire mixture is utilized.

VI

Aval Puttu

Aval is one of the favorite food for Lord Krishna. Aval Puttu is one of the simple sweet that we can make for an offering to Lord Krishna. Aval Puttu is made using Aval (Poha), Jaggery and grated coconut and seasoned with cashews.

Recipe:

Ingredients:

- Aval (Poha) – 1 cup
- Jaggery – ½ cup
- Grated coconut – ¼ cup
- Cardamom Powder – ½ tsp.
- Cashew nuts – 10 Nos
- Ghee – 4 tsp.

Method :

- Dry fry the poha in a kadai till it turns light brown. Cool and grind it to a fine powder.
- Put this powder in a big bowl and sprinkle little warm water and mix well. If you hold the flour in your palm and press, it should be like a ball and put it back, it should fall loosely like puttu flour. Keep aside.
- In another vessel, put the jaggery and add ¼ cup water and bring to boil.
- Remove and strain it. Again put it back on the stove and allow to boil for five minutes or till reaches one string consistency.

- Add coconut gratings and the poha powder and immediately switch off the stove. Mix well.
- Add cardamom powder, ghee and fried cashew nuts and once again mix well.
- Keep it covered for at least half – an – hour and then serve.

VII

Awan Bangwi

It is special type of cake made only by Tripuri. The special type of leaf used for preparing this cake is *Lairu*. Apart from it, banana leaf can also be used. Or nowadays thick aluminum foil has also been used successfully. Many variety of *bangwi* are prepared, viz. plain bangwi, only with guria rice, onion and ginger; Cashew nut–Resin bangwi with added nut, resin, and ghee in it; Pork Bangwi, addition of small pieces of pork and lard in it etc. and one can make different types of combination as per choices.

Recipe:

Ingredients:

- Mami rice– 2 kg.
- Lairu leaves– 25 pc.
- Ginger– 150gms
- Cashew nuts– 200 gms
- Ghee or butter oil– 200 gms
- Resins – 100gms.

Method:

- Soak the Mami rice for 4–5 hours.
- Peel off the ginger, chop it finely.
- Separate each half of cashew nuts in two.
- Soak the resins for 1–2 hours.
- Wash and clean the lairu leaves, and soak the canes in water.
- Sieve the Mami rice and transfer it in a big container.

- Mix the chopped ginger with rice, and then mix the halved cashew nuts.
- Now add the ghee or butter oil in it and thoroughly mix it.
- Take one leaf of lairu, make a cone of it, keeping the end part of leaves inside.
- With help of spoon, pour mixed rice in cone, and fill 4/5 th of the cone,
- Fold down the upper end of leaf and tie around it with the cane. It will look a cone shaped ice cream.
- This way make bangwi out of all 2 kg it will make some 18–22 piece of bangwi depending on size of cone.
- Now cover it and boil it in a big container till cooked, drain the water out.
- Then peel of the leaves and serve the bangwi warm or hot.
- One more way of making it tastier is to roast the cooked bangwi in grill till it turns light brown, and then peel of leaves to serve hot.

VIII

Bal Mithai

Bal Mithai is brown chocolate–like fudge, made with roasted khoa, coated with white sugar balls, and is a popular sweet from Almora, Nainital and Bageshwar in the Himalayan state of Uttarakhand in India, especially regions around Almora. It is one of the most favourite sweet of common people and the people living near Almora region.

Bal Mithai, which sneaked into the Kumaon region of the Central Himalayas from Nepal– in all probability around 7–8th century AD, when Sun worship was quite prevalent in hills. Scholars of Assyriology say that 'bal' happened to be the name of Sun God in ancient Assyrian culture and initially must have been the name of the prime offering to the Sun God. Sun worship died in Kumaon several centuries ago, but not the bal mithai.

Bal Mithai was again rejuvenated by of Lala Joga Ram Shah of Lal Bazaar, Almora during early twentieth century.

Recipe:

Ingredients:

- Fresh khoya / mawa– 500 gram
- Cocoa powder– 2 tbsp
- Sugar powder– ½ cup
- Desi ghee – 1 tbsp
- Bal dana / sugar balls– 4 tbsp
- Sugar– ½ cup
- Water– ¼ cup

Method:

- Take Mawa & grate it in a plate
- Heat Ghee in thick bottom kadai or nonstick pan, keep the flame low
- Add Mawa & stir it till mawa leaves the ghee, add cocoa powder & mix it well.
- Add sugar powder and mix it well, keep stirring till it become thick, Switch off the flame.
- Now take a plate and grease it with ghee.
- Put batter in a plate, level it with help of knife.
- Keep it aside for one hour to cool down
- After one hour cut into small square or rectangular burfi like pieces per your choice, again keep it aside to cool down further.
- In another pan add sugar and water, mix it well.
- Keep boiling till it becomes little thick, Keep is aside for cooling.
- Now take Barfi pieces, dip in sugar syrup and coat it with Bal Dana (sugar balls) all over
- Place the Barfi in serving plate and repeat the same with every piece. Bal mithai is ready.

Note –If you don't get Bal Dana or Sugar Balls you can use non medicated homeopathic sugar balls too.

IX

Balushahi

This is a traditional dessert in northern Indian Cuisine, Pakistani Cuisine, Nepali cuisine, and Bangladeshi cuisine. It is similar to a glazed doughnut in terms of ingredients, but differs in texture and taste. In South India, a similar pastry is known as *Badushah*. Balushahi has a soft texture from outside, whereas a Badushah has a crisp texture from outside. Balushahis are made of maida flour, and are deep–fried in clarified butter and then dipped in sugar syrup. Balushahi is typically made during Diwali and other festive occasions. In the north of India, especially in the Punjabi community, this sweet is a must at a marriage.

The exact historical fact to support the origin of this sweet is not well known, but the

—*shahi*‖ indicated in the name suggests that this dish has some origin with the Persians, and then carried over by the Mughals from north to south India. The

—*Shahi*‖ cuisine is also incredibly rich usually, and the Balushahi is nothing if not rich considering the ghee in it! Also, the deep–fried pastry dipped in sugar syrup is reminiscent of sweets from the Middle East.

Recipe:

Ingredients:

- Refined flour (maida) – 1 ½ cups
- Soda bicarbonate – ¼ tsp
- Ghee – 4 tbsps
- Yogurt whisked – 6 tbsps
- Sugar – 2 cups

- Milk – 2 tbsps
- Pistachios finely chopped – 4–5

Method:

- Sift together the flour and soda bicarbonate into a large bowl. Rub four tbsps of ghee into the flour mixture with your fingertips till it resembles breadcrumbs.
- Add the beaten yogurt and knead into soft dough. Cover the dough with a damp cloth and allow it to rest for forty–five minutes.
- Divide the dough into twelve equal portions and shape into smooth balls. Take care not to overwork the dough. Make a slight dent in the centre of the ball with your thumb. Keep the balls covered.
- Heat sufficient ghee in a non–stick kadai on medium heat. Gently slide in the prepared dough balls, two to three at a time, and deep–fry on low heat. If necessary, place a non–stick tawa below the kadai so that the ghee does not get too hot.
- Gradually the Balushahis will start floating to the top. Turn gently and fry the other side till golden. The entire process may take around half an hour to forty–five minutes. Remove with a slotted spoon and drain on absorbent paper. Set aside to cool for forty–five minutes, or till they reach room temperature.
- Cook the sugar with one cup of water in a deep non–stick pan on high heat, stirring occasionally, till the sugar dissolves. Add the milk to the cooking syrup. Collect the scum which rises to the surface with a ladle and discard. Continue to cook till the syrup attains a two–string consistency.
- Remove the syrup from heat and soak the cooled Balushahis in it for two hours.
- Gently remove the Balushahis from the sugar syrup and place on a serving plate. Decorate with the pistachios. Set aside for two to three hours till the sugar syrup forms a thin white coating on the Balushahis.

X

Barfi

Barfi, borfi or burfi is a dense milk–based sweet from the Indian subcontinent, and a type of mithai. The name is a derivative of the Persian word *Barf*, which means snow. This is due to the white colour it has in its most simple form. Every barfi maker has their own versions of the recipe. Traditionally, barfi was made with milk that was cooked slowly until the liquid was reduced to a fudge–like consistency.

This milk solid was then flavoured with either saffron, vanilla essence, cardamom or rose water. Depending on type of barfi being prepared, cashews, almonds, pistachios or fresh coconut were added. A few of the famous varieties of barfi include *Besan barfi* (made with gram flour), *Kaaju barfi* (made with cashews), *Pista barfi* (made with ground pistachios), *Sing barfi* (made with peanuts) and *Koprapak* (made with coconut). The main ingredients of plain barfis include khoya, sugar and small cardamom. The ingredients are cooked in a vessel until the mixture solidifies. Adding edible silver leaf (*vark*) to the edges of barfi is common when the sweet confection is served at a wedding. For added flavour and to provide a colourful contrast, often it is rolled in crushed nuts before being served. They are typically cut into square, diamond, or round shapes. The sweet is easily adapted for casual occasions to the most formal event. Different types of barfi vary in their colour and texture. The confection is served in Pakistan and India, all year round, but especially consumed during the holiday seasons, wedding ceremonies, and religious festivals. Barfi is often served during Eid and also Diwali.

Recipe of common Barfi:

Ingredients:

- Unsweetened khoya–250 gms.
- Sugar–5 tbsp
- Powdered gr. cardamoms –4
- Finely chopped pistachios–15
- Finely chopped almonds or cashews–15
- Saffron–a pinch (optional)
- Milk–1 to 1.5 tsp (optional)
- Ghee–¼ to 1/3 tsp for greasing the pan or tray

Method:

- First grate or crumble the unsweetened khoya.
- In a small bowl dissolve a few saffron strands in 1 tsp of milk. This is an optional step.
- Grease a bit of ghee, on a butter paper lined on a tray or on a thali/tray.
- Add the grated khoya in a thick bottomed pan.
- Begin to cook on a low flame for 2 to 3 minutes stirring often.
- Switch off the flame and add sugar.
- Stir. Then turn on the flame. The whole mixture's consistency will become smooth and slightly thin, due to the sugar getting melted.
- Stir often and continue to cook on a low flame.
- When the mixture becomes slightly thick and starts leaving the sides of the pan, as you see in the pic in step number 9, its time for the next step.
- Avoid cooking too much as then the barfi will have a chewy texture. The time taken to get this texture right from the time, sugar is added is about 8 to 9 minutes on a low flame. The time will vary a couple of minutes here and there, depending on the size, type, quality of the pan and intensity of the flame.
- Add chopped dry fruits (almonds, pistachios) or your choice of dry fruits. Also add cardamom powder.
- Stir and cook for a minute. Switch off the flame.
- Pour the entire barfi mixture in the greased pan or butter paper.
- Spread evenly keeping 1 inch thickness at the edges.
- Sprinkle the saffron scented milk on the burfi.
- Once the barfi cools down, slice into squares or diamond shapes.
- Serve barfi immediately. You can also store them in an airtight box. These barfi stay good for about 4 to 5 days in the refrigerator.

XI

Basundi

Basundi is sweet thickened milk, flavored with cardamom and nutmeg, with the addition of dry fruits, especially popular in Western Indian states of Gujarat and Maharashtra during the festivals of Rakshabandhan, Janmashtami Kali Chaudas and Bhaubeej (*Bhai Dooj*). It is a sweetened condensed milk made by boiling milk on low heat until the milk is reduced by half. In North India, a similar dish goes by the name rabri. Different styles of basundi are also prepared, such as *sitaphal* (custard apple) *basundi* and *angoor basundi* (basundi with smaller kinds of rasogullas.

Recipe:

Ingredients:

- Milk, full cream– 2 litre
- Cashew / kaju, chopped– 2 tbsp
- Sugar– ½ cup
- Almonds / badam, chopped– 2 tbsp
- Pistachios, chopped– 2 tbsp
- Saffron / kesar– ¼ tsp
- Cardamom powder / elachi powder– ¼ tsp

Method:

- Firstly, in a large thick bottomed kadai boil 2–litre milk stirring occasionally.
- Once the milk comes to a boil, add 2 tbsp chopped cashew, almonds and pistachios.

- Stir well making sure milk doesn't stick to the bottom.
- Boil the milk on low flame for 30 minutes or till milk reduces.
- Keep stirring in between to avoid sticking till the milk reduces to quarter.
- Now add ½ cup sugar and ¼ tsp saffron and mix well.
- Boil for another 5 minutes or till the milk thickens completely.
- Now add ¼ tsp cardamom powder and mix well.
- Finally, serve Basundi chilled or hot garnished with few dry fruits.

XII

Bebinca

Bebinca, also known as bibik or bebinka, is a type of pudding and a traditional Indo– Portuguese dessert. *Traditionally it is also* called *"The queen of Goan desserts,"* is a seven– to sixteen–layer pudding cake made from incrementally–baked sheets. This is a must–have at any celebration in Goa. The ingredients include plain flour, sugar, ghee (clarified butter), egg yolk, and coconut milk. Traditionaly it was made by using Dum method of cooking put a coconut shell or charcoal on the top of the sinni (cover) but now a days people used to prepare it in Salamander. Legend says that Bebinca was made by a nun called Bibiona of the convento da Santa Monica in old Goa. She made it with seven layers to symbolize the seven hills of Lisbon and old Goa and offered it to the priest. But he found it too small and thus the layers were increased. Ideally it is 14 and 16 layers.

Recipe:

Ingredients:

- Thick coconut milk (the first extract of coconut milk)– 250 ml
- Yolks–6 egg
- Refined flour–175 gms
- Desi ghee–1 tbsp
- Desi ghee for the bibinca batter–½ cup
- Sugar–200 gms
- Nutmeg powder–1 tsp
- Cardamom powder–1 tsp
- Almonds– few flaked
- Vanilla essence (optional)–1 tbsp

- Salt–a pinch

Method:

- Preheat oven to 180°C exactly fifteen minutes before baking. Grease a round tin Or loaf pan with 2 tbsp ghee.
- Take a mixing vessel, combine coconut milk and sugar. With the help of electric beater beat until sugar dissolves.
- Add one egg yolk at a time and beat until they all mix nicely.
- Now add flour, 1 tbsp ghee and salt. Beat all nicely.
- Pour ½ cup of batter and bake for 25 mins.
- Allow to cool completely. Unmould the pan gently with a tap from behind. Slice bibinca and serve warm or cold with a dollop of ice-cream.
- For the last batter spread ghee, sprinkle, cardamom, nutmeg and vanilla essence if using. Add flaked almonds if using now. Bake the last layer for 20– 22 mins.
- Continue greasing and baking with ½ cup batter until all batter is finished. Bake each layer for fifteen minutes.
- Bake again for fifteen mins. Again spread ghee, cardamom powder and vanilla essence.
- Now spread some ghee over it with the help of brush. Sprinkle little cardamom powder and vanilla essence if using.

XIII
Boorelu

Boorelu, Poornam boorelu or Poornalu is a traditional and popularsweet of Andhra Pradesh and Telangana. This golden sweet ball or dumplings have a yummy Poornam (mixture of chana dal/ urad/mixed dal paste, jaggery, cardamom and dry nuts) inside which is covered by a rice dough and fried in oil. Often Poornalu is served along with ghee to enhance its flavor.

Poornalu is mostly served during festivals, weddings & other special occasions after the main course and rarely as an evening snack in most Telugu households. Most telugu speaking homes prepare poornam boorelu for *Varalakshmi vratham & Durga navratri* to offer as Naivedyam to the Goddess. These are then shared with family, friends & neighbors.Preferably it is better consumed hot. It is made in abundance during the famous Makar Sankranti – the festival of harvest. During this time, poornalu is made exuberantly and most heartily and distributed among friends, relatives and neighbours. Poornalu is often served at weddings and other festivities. The preparation and serving of Poornalu, however, undergoes minor alterations from place to place.Poornalu are commonly prepared Poornalu are also made in other neighboring states are known as Sukhiyan in malayalam, Suyam, Suzhiyan or Sugunta in other regional languages.

Recipe:

Ingredients:

- Urad Dal–1 cup
- Rice1–½ cup
- Chana Dal or Bengal Gram–1 cup
- Jaggery–3/4 or 1 cup
- Cardamom–2 pods
- Salt–½ tbsp
- Oil–to deep fry

Method:

- Wash and soak urad dal and rice for 4–5hrs or overnight. Grind them to a fine batter like a thick dosa batter. Add salt, mix well and keep aside.
- Wash and soak chana dal for 2 hrs or overnight. Add the soaked chana dal to pressure cooker, add 1½ cups water or just up to the level of dal and pressure cook for 4 to 5 whistles.
- When the pressure goes off, check whether dal is cooked nicely. If any water is left over, remove the lid and cook for few more minutes to drain the water completely.
- Now smash the dal with a spoon or spatula. Dal should be smooth if not you can also blend to smooth.
- Add 3/4 or 1 cup of jaggery to the dal. Here I have mixed 3/4 cup if you like more sweet you can add 1 cup.
- Keep on stirring till the jaggery melts and nicely mixes with dal on low flame. Add cardamom powder and mix well.
- When the water evaporates and the dal is dry, switch off the flame and cool the dal completely.
- When the dal is cooled completely, make a small lemon size balls and set aside.
- Meanwhile heat the oil in a deep frying pan. When the oil is hot enough, take one ball, dip it in the batter and drop it in the oil.
- Repeat the process for the other balls and fry them on medium flame till golden.
- Drain them on the kitchen towel. Serve hot.

XIV

Cham cham

It is also known as chom chom or chum chum. It is one of the other Bengali delicacies apart from Rasgulla, Sandesh and Rasmalai that can be found in Indian Sweet shops. Cham cham sweet is made with lot of fancy colorful stuffings and garnishing.

This sweet is made by curdling milk and then shaping the coagulated solids to cylindrical or oblong pieces pieces. These are cooked in sugar syrup similar to rasgullas to get soft, spongy and light texture. The sweet is then garnished with mawa or coconut scrapping or nuts.

It is made during Durga puja or Diwali. The history of Porabari chamcham, an oval – shaped brownish variety of chomchom from Porabari in Tangail District of modern – day Bangladesh, dates back to mid – 19th century. The modern version of this dish was made by Matilal Gore, based on a sweet dish prepared by his grandfather Raja Ram Gore, who was a native of Ballia district in Uttar Pradesh, India.

Recipe:

Ingredients:

For chenna:

- Full cream cows milk – 4 cups
- Vinegar or lemon juice – 2 tbsp
- Maida – 1 tbsp

For sugar syrup:

- Sugar – 1½ cup

- Water – 8 cups
- Gr.cardamom – 2 pods

For stuffing:

- Ghee – 1 tsp
- Milk – ¼ cup
- Cream – 2 tbsp
- Milk powder – ½ cup
- Saffron milk – 2 tbsp
- Powdered sugar – 1 tbsp

Other ingredients:

- Desiccated coconut – ¼ cup
- Tutti frutti – 3 tbsp

Method:

- Firstly, prepare chenna by curdling milk. Drain completely.
- And hang for 30 minutes.
- After 30 minutes, start to knead the paneer for 8 minutes.
- Additionally add 1 tbsp maida and combine well.
- Furthermore, make small oval balls of paneer.
- Boil for 15 minutes in sugar syrup.
- Furthermore, keep aside till it cools completely.
- Take cooked paneer balls leaving behind the water.
- Slit in between and stuff sweetened khoya.
- Further, roll them in desiccated coconut.
- And garnish with tutti frutti or dry fruits of your choice.
- Finally, serve chum chum recipe immediately or store in refrigerator.

XV
Chhannar Payesh

Chhannar Payesh is an authentic dessert recipe of Bengali cuisine for special occasions and festivals. Also known as cottage cheese pudding or paneer kheer, this is an exotic and classic sweet dish which is quite popular during the New year celebration and other festive season. The best thing about this kheer recipe is that you don't need to add sugar in it, it is prepared using condensed milk which itself is sweet enough to make the dish taste sweeter. This dessert recipe is cooked using paneer or cottage cheese, milk, condensed milk, and uses green cardamom powder that enhances the taste and flavour of this mouth – watering dish.

Recipe:

Ingredients:

- Home made paneer – 3/4 cup (Needs to be fresh)
- Milk – 4 cups
- Sugar – 3/4 cup (or more as per preference)
- Saffron – a pinch soaked in a tablespoon of milk
- Cardamom Powder – ½ tsp
- Mixed nuts – ½ cup

Optional ingredients:

- Condensed milk can be used to make it richer and thicker and also to reduce the cooking time.
- Corn Flour / Rice Flour can be used as a thickening agent

Method:

- Knead the fresh paneer well and make small roundels of them and set aside.
- Boil milk under a reduced flame until it is reduced to 1/2 or 3/4 of its quantity. Add sugar and the saffron. Take care to make sure the milk doesn't get burnt. So continuous stirring is a good idea.
- Gently drop the prepared paneer balls into the simmering milk. Let it simmer for a few more minutes.
- Remove and refrigerate upon cooling and serve.

XVI
Chhena Gaja

Chhena gaja is a sweet signature dish from Odisha, India. Unlike some other popular chhena–based Oria desserts, such as rasagola, which have spread throughout India, the Chhena gaja remains largely popular within the state itself. It is the village of Pahala that excels in making this sweet.Although the ingredients of chhena gaja are essentially the same as that of rasagolla and chhena poda, the dishes are very different in taste.

Chhena gajas are prepared by combining chhena, similar to cottage cheese, and sooji (semolina), and kneading the dough thoroughly. Water is squeezed out from the mixture, which is then dried briefly until it acquires the right consistency. It is then molded into palm–sized rectangular shapes (gajas), boiled in thick sugar syrup. Sometimes, the gajas are then allowed to dry a little more, in which case the sugar may occasionally crystallize on the surface.

Recipe:

Ingredients:

For Chhena:

- Full Fat Milk–1 litre
- Lemon Juice–1tbsp
- Ice–6 to 8 cubes

For Sugar Syrup:

- Sugar–½ cup
- Water–2/3 cup
- Lemon Juice–½tsp
- Rose Water Or Few Drops of Kewra–1–2 tbsp

Other Ingredients

- Semolina–1 tbsp
- Oil or Ghee for Frying

Method:

Making Chhena:

- Bring the milk to a boil.
- Turn off the heat and wait for 2 to 3 minutes.
- Now add the lemon juice gradually and stir till the whey separates from the milk solids.
- Add the ice cubes and wait for 5 minutes.
- Using a thin cotton cloth or cheese cloth, drain all the whey from the Chhena.
- Wash the Chhena well under running water to remove traces of the lemon.
- Squeeze the extra water from the Chhena.

Making the Sugar Syrup:

- In a heavy–bottomed vessel, combine the sugar and water.
- Now cook these ingredients till you get thick syrup (one string consistency).
- Add a few drops of lemon juice and mix well. This prevents the sugar syrup from crystallizing after we take it off the heat.
- Add the rose water and mix well.
- Over low flame, keep the sugar syrup remain warm.

Making the Gaja:

- Break up the Chhena till it is crumbly.

- Add the rava and knead well till it comes together as smooth dough.
- Divide the dough into 8 to 12 equal portions.
- Roll each portion into a ball and then press to form a disc.
- Shape the disc into a square.
- Set aside. Cover with a damp cloth, if required.
- In a small kadhai, over low flame, heat about ½ cup of oil.
- To test the heat of the oil, add a tiny ball of chhena to the oil. It should sizzle on the surface of the oil.
- Keeping the heat at low to medium, add a few Gaja at a time to the oil and fry till golden brown.
- Using a slotted spoon, remove the Gaja from the oil and add to the Sugar Syrup.
- Fry all the Gaja, and add them to the sugar syrup.
- Let the Chhena Gaja soak in the syrup for about 1 hour.
- Remove the Chhena Gaja from the syrup and serve.

XVII

Chhena Jhili

Chhena jhili is a popular dessert from Cuisine of Odisha. The birthplace is Nimapada in Puri district. It is prepared in fried cheese and sugar syrup. This special sweet (a deep fried cottage cheese patty) is prepared with fried cheese, cardamom powder, ghee and sugar syrup. It is best eaten hot to feel the soft, juicy cheesiness with the backdrop of a little cardamom flavor. The extraordinary fried flavor with the touch of sweet make it more special. The man who started preparing this sweet was Aartabandhu Sahoo from the Shyam Sundarpur Village of Nimapara. It was started from Puri the sacred land of lord jagannatha, just in a few years it spreads all over the odisha and abroad also.

Recipe:

Ingredients:

- Fresh Chhena/ Cottage Cheese – 400gm
- Pure Ghee/ Oil – 500ml
- Wheat Flour – 2 tsp
- Sugar – 2 tsp
- Cardamom Powder – 1/2 tsp
- Semolina – 1 tsp
- Salt – Pinch

For Sugar Syrup:

- Water – 500 ml
- Sugar – 500 gm

Method:

- Take a bowl. Make a soft dough by mixing Chhena, wheat flour, semolina, sugar, elaichi powder and a pinch of salt into it.
- On a flat surface knead the dough using your palm very well to get a smooth texture. Remember for this recipe, kneading is a very important process which will take approximately 15 – 20 mins.
- Apply little oil in palm. Make small balls out of this dough and flatten these into thick patties. If at that time breaking or cracking occurs, then I would suggest you to knead more.
- Now keep these cheese balls separately in a bowl and cover it with a lid for sometimes.
- To prepare Sugar Syrup all you need is some Water and Sugar. Take same amount of water and sugar to prepare the sugar syrup. Stir it and boil this for 10 mins to make a thick syrup and now add some cardamom powder to it.
- Now take another heating wok filled with Ghee or Oil (Ghee is more recommended) and deep fry the balls until the color turns into beautiful and rich dark brown color.
- Once it done, remove it and straightway add it to the hot sugar syrup. Stir it again and let it soak for 4 – 5 hours.
- You can add some dry fruits and elaichi to garnish it and serve.

XVIII

Chhena Murki

Chhena murki, or chenna murki, is a sweet made from an Indian version of cottage cheese, milk and sugar in many states such as Odisha. Milk and sugar are boiled to a thick consistency and round, cube, cuboid or other shapes of cottage cheese are soaked in the milky condensate. The sweet originated in the coastal areas in the district of Bhadrak and nowadays is available in all parts of Odisha. Other flavors and aromatic spices are typically added. It is also known by Bengali and Guyanese people as Pera.

Recipe:

Ingredients:

- Paneer – 250 gms
- Sugar – 1 cup (250 gms)
- Green Cardamom – 4
- Rose water – 1 tsp

Method:

- Take paneer and cut into small pieces. Take small cardamoms. Peel and coarsely grind them.
- Take a nonstick pan add 1 cup sugar to it also add ½ cup water, turn on the flame. Stir well. Keep a check on the sugar syrup. Cook for 2 minutes. To check the sugar syrup, pour a few drops of syrup in a bowl and let it cool. Keep the flame low. Stick a little syrup on your fingers and check. If it forms a single thread on cooling then the syrup is ready.

- Put the paneer pieces to the sugar syrup, add cardamom powder too. Cook on low flame until the sugar syrup reaches the setting consistency. Keep stirring regularly so that there is even coating over the paneer.
- Once the sugar syrup is transparent and reaches the setting consistency then turn off the flame. Lift the pan and place on a jali stand. Add 1 tsp rosewater and constantly stir it. Cool it while stirring it.

XIX

Chhena Poda

Chhena poda is delectable, heavenly and extremely popular sweet made of cottage cheese from Odisha. Its literally means burnt cheese in Odia language. It is made of well–kneaded homemade fresh cheese chhena, sugar is baked for several hours until it browns. Chhena poda is the only well known Indian dessert whose flavor is predominantly derived from the caramelization of sugar. Chhenapoda originated in the Odia town of Nayagarh in the first half of the twentieth century. The owner of a confectionery, Sudarshana Sahu decided to add sugar and seasonings to leftover cottage cheese one night, and left it in an oven that was still warm from earlier use. The next day, he was pleasantly surprised to find out what a scrumptious dessert he had created. Chenna Poda is used in all functions, including marriages and other celebrations. It is also associated with the Jagannath temple and is offered to the Lord Jagannath. It is also popular in Dussera. This is an easy–to–make sweet dish which is prepared using paneer, semolina, raisins, cashews, ghee and sugar and baked to dark brown coloured crust.

Recipe:

Ingredients:

- Paneer or cottage cheese – 2 cup, crumbled
- Sugar – ½ cup + 2 tbsp
- Cardamom powder – 1 tsp
- Cashew nuts – 2 tbsp
- Raisins – 2 tbsp
- Milk or whey – 4 tbsp

- Ghee or butter – for greasing
- Sugar – for caramelization
- Pistachio – to garnish

Method:

- Preheat the oven at 180°.
- Fry cashew nuts and raisins lightly.
- Blend paneer or cottage cheese, sugar and cardamom powder. Mix well.
- Add milk or remaining whey of paneer. Blend till the mixture becomes smooth. Taste and adjust sugar if required. I like less sweet.
- Add fried cashew nuts and raisins. Mix well.
- Grease a baking pan with ghee or butter. Spread 1 tbsp sugar and heat the pan till sugar caramelize.
- When sugar caramelized switch off the flame.
- Tilt the pan to spread the caramelized syrup all over the base.
- Pour the paneer mixture over it.
- Spread evenly with a spoon or spatula.
- Bake in a preheated oven at 180° for 35 – 45 minutes.
- To check insert a toothpick in the middle. If the toothpick comes out clean chhena poda is ready.
- Take out the pan when hot and invert it on a plate to take out.
- If it becomes cold sugar syrup at base will be hard and it will be difficult to come out intact.
- Garnish with pistachio. Serve delicious chhena poda or baked cottage cheese hot or cold.

XX Chikki

Chikki is a traditional Indian sweet (brittle) generally made rom nuts and jaggery/sugar. There are several different varieties of chikki in addition to the most common groundnut (peanut) chikki. Each variety of chikki is named after the ingredients used, which include puffed or roasted Bengal gram, sesame, puffed rice, beaten rice, or khobra (desiccated coconut), and other nuts such as almonds, cashews and pistachios. In regions of North India, especially Bihar and Uttar Pradesh, this sweet is called *Layiya patti*. In Sindh and Sindhi regions of India, it is called Layer or Lai and in other north Indian states, it is also known as *gajar* or *Maroond*ah. In Bangladesh, it is known as *Gur badam*. In South Indian states of Telangana and Andhra Pradesh, it is called *Palli Patti*. Similar dishes are also very popular in Brazil, where it is known as *pé–de–moleque*, and in Paraguay, where it is called *Ka'í Ladrillo*. Some chikkis are made using a combination of ingredients. Special chikkis are made out of cashews, almonds, and pistachios also sesame seed called *Ellu* in Tamil. Though jaggery is the usual sweetener material, sugar is used as the base in certain types of chikkis. It is a very popular sweet item in both rural and urban South Asia (spanning India, Pakistan, Bangladesh, Nepal and Sri Lanka). Some also add glucose to the chikkis, which are usual there. It started from a single flavor of jaggery and peanuts. And today there are different exotic flavors such as strawberry, cranberry available in the market.

In the South Indian state of Tamil Nadu, the preparation is with a larger proportion of nuts to jaggery and the mixture is formed into balls and slabs. The most common versions are *Kadalai Urundai* (peanut balls), *Ellu Urundai* (sesame balls) and *Pori Urundai* (puffed rice balls). In Kerala, it is made in both slab and ball forms. Peanut based sweet is called as *Kadala Mithai* or *Kappalandi Mithai* or in some places as *Abhayaarthi Katta* . And the sesame based sweet is called as *Ellunda*. Lonavla, the hill station in the Indian state of Maharashtra is synonymous with Chikki; no trip is complete without tourists picking up a few packets of their favourite chikki to take back home.

Recipe of Common Chikki:

Ingredients:

- Peanuts–1 cup
- Jaggery–150 gms.
- Water–1 tbsp
- Ghee (or coconut oil)–1 tsp

Method:

- Roast peanuts on a medium to low flame stirring often until deep golden and aromatic.
- To check remove the skin and look for golden color on the nut. This deep roasting brings out a nutty aroma from peanuts.
- Cool and de-skin them.
- Take a cup and gently rub the nuts with the base of the cup.
- Transfer them to a plate and crush them randomly with the base of the cup for 2 to 3 mins. This will crush the peanuts a bit and bring out the nutty aroma of the peanuts. Keep this aside.
- Grease a steel plate with little ghee. Set this aside.
- Next grease a rolling pin or the base of a cup to level the hot chikki mixture.
- Keep a small bowl half filled with water ready to check the consistency of jaggery syrup.
- Grate the jaggery and add to a heavy bottom pan. Pour just 1 tbsp water. Begin to dissolve on a low flame.
- When it dissolves completely, remove the impurities.
- Add ghee and mix. Boil the jaggery syrup until it reaches a hard ball brittle consistency (three strings).
- Lower the flame completely.
- To check hard ball brittle consistency, drop little jaggery syrup to the bowl of water. It must become hard immediately.
- Add the peanuts and mix well.

- Quickly pour this to the steel plate. With the help of a spatula, shape to a rectangle.
- Roll the mixture with the rolling pin evenly. Within a minute it will set, so you must be fast. Cut to pieces, when it is still slightly hot.
- Cool completely and break the peanut chikki to pieces.
- Store in an air tight jar.

XXI
Danadar

Danadar is a very popular sweet of West Bengal. It is a drier form of Rasogolla or Rasgulla Sweets, Chum Chum sweet, and Rajbhog sweets. This sweet is easy to make and crunchy in texture. It is dry with syrup still clinging on the outside; or rather dried sugar crystals are formed. Unlike the Rasgulla, where the sugar syrup is mild, this sugar syrup is thick and it is 1 – 1 ratio of sugar to water. Once you boil the chhana in the preferred shape, it is then cooked further in the sugar syrup until it gets completely coated and dry. In the end, you will end up having a crunchy sweet, with a thick sugar layer coating it.

Recipe:

Ingredients:

- Milk – 1 liter
- Sooji – 1 tsp
- Flour – 1 tsp
- Sugar – 2 Cup
- Cardamom Powder – ½ Tsp
- Lemon juice – as required
- Water – as required

Method:

- Boil milk, add lemon juice gradually and stir well. The milk will curdle. Rest for 10 minutes.

- Strain the curdled milk through muslin cloth, squeeze excess water from chhana / chenna (cottage cheese). Keep a side.
- Wash and rinse the chhana / chenna (cottage cheese)/ with cold water to remove sourness from chhana. Again squeeze excess water from chhana. Keep a side.
- Take a steel flat plate. Place the chhana add cardamom powder and mix it well.
- Knead it very well for about 20 minutes with help of palm of hands. Make soft dough from the chhana / chenna (cottage cheese).
- Divide into small equal size balls and make a cylindrical shape. Keep a side.
- Take a wok with 2 cups of water. Next add 2 cup of sugar and mix it very well. Increase to heat to dissolve the sugar.
- Add chhana ball into the hot water. (reduce to heat medium). Cover the wok. Cook for 5 minutes.
- After 5 minutes, open the cover. Flip the Danadar to other sides very carefully. You can notice that now increase the Danadar size double. Cover the wok again. Cook for 10 minutes. Reduce to heat very low.
- After 10 minutes, open the cover. When sugar syrup is very thick and dry in consistency. Then switch off the flame.
- Take out Danadar very carefully from the sugar syrup. Remove the excess syrup. Keep aside for about 4 to 6 hours. Allow to cool or keep the Danadar sweets into of the Refrigerator or fridge.
- Serve the Danadar at room temperature or cold.

XXII
Dehrori

Dehrori is one of the unique and popular traditional sweet of *Chhattisgarh and it is commonly prepared in every house during festivals like Holi and Diwali.* The origin of Dehrori is from Chhattisgarh yet it is dissipated in different states as well. It is a sweet delicacy and heavenly which is normally arranged during the festive period of Holi and Diwali. It is the sweet ball which is deep fried, covered with jaggery syrup. Dehrori is made with batter of rice flour (New rice which is freshly harvested in the month of November) and curd which is fermented overnight and then mixed with ghee, sugar, cardamom powder, and nuts (your choice). After that it is deep fried dipped in jaggeryor sugar syrup. Its preparation actually takes more than a day, and so it is kind of special. *It is also acknowledged as "Rice Gulab Jamun".* The flavor of Dehrori is sweet and marginally tartish and its surface is to some degree hard and granular because of the rice flour.

Recipe:

Ingredients:

- Rice –1 cup
- Water – ¼ cup
- Yogurt – ¼ cup
- Ghee – ½ cup for frying
- Sugar – 2 cups
- Cardamom powder – 2 tsp
- Nuts – to garnish

Method:

- Rinse and soak the rice in water for approximately 6 hours. You can take any variety of rice.
- After 6 hours drain the water completely from the rice and blend coarsely, it should look like sooji. Make sure there is no water while you blend.
- To the blended rice, add yogurt and mix with hands. Mix till the batter receives the warmth from your palms. Do not add anything to the batter.
- Cover and leave the batter overnight for fermentation. Fermentation provides fluffiness in the batter and the dumplings get cooked easily while frying.
- Next day, prepare sugar syrup by adding water and sugar and cook till 1 string consistency. You can check the string by taking the syrup between thumb and index finger. Switch off the flame and add cardamom powder. Keep it aside.
- Heat ghee in a high flame first, then reduce the flame to medium. Make dumplings out of the fermented batter and fry gently. Once the dumplings get light brown in color on both sides, place it in paper towels to remove excess oil and then dip them in the warm sugar syrup. Let it dip till it is nicely soaked in sugar syrup.
- Garnish it with the choice of nuts.

XXIII

Dharwad Peda

Dharwad Peda is a unique delicacy from North Karnataka. The name —Dharwad‖ has been derived from a place called Dharwad which has a history of this sweet since 150 Years. The sweet was discovered by a Ram Ratan Singh Thakur Family from Uttar Pradesh. Traditionally the sweet is prepared from buffalo's milk that are raised by the Gavali community in and around Dharwad.The pedhas that he made and sold became so popular that the street on which the shop stands came to be known as *Line Bazaar*– easily identified by the ever present queue of people waiting to make a purchase. This light brown coloured peda is garnished with sugar giving its traditional appeal. The much awarded pedha, from the Lord Willingdon Medal in 1913 to the Priyadarshini Indira Gandhi Award in 2001 and 2013 and the Rajiv Gandhi Excellence Award in 2002 and 2013, is today an intrinsic part of the history, culture and traditions of our country. Mathura Pedha is the parent of this local popular sweet dish.

Recipe:

Ingredients:

- Khoya–2 cups
- Ghee–10 –15 gms
- Finely powdered sugar– 1½ cup
- Freshly ground green cardamom powder–a pinch
- Mace powder–a pinch
- Clove powder–a pinch

Method:

- Add grated khoya in a heavy bottom pan and start cooking.
- Add ghee in small amounts to keep the mixture moist.
- Keep stirring continuously on a low to medium flame. Keep an eye on the khoya and ensure it doesn't burn. This is really the _make or break' step in making the perfect Dharwad Pedha.
- When the colour of khoya turns brown, add sugar and stir.
- Add the spices and let it cool.
- Take bite–sized quantities of khoya mix and make them into pedhas.
- Roll them over some powdered sugar till you get a thin layer.

XXIV
Dhondas

This is a popular Konkani sweet which is also called Tavsale in Goa. Generally prepared using dark green cucumber that you get in rainy season. But you can also make this using light green cucumber that are generally available all through the year. This steamed sweet cake gets its lovely grainy texture with semolina and grated cucumber and sweetness from jaggery. The mixture is baked like a cake.

Recipe:

Ingredients:

- Grated Cucumber–3 cups
- Rawa/Suji–2 cups
- Jaggery–2 cups
- Freshly grated coconut–2 cups
- Green cardamom powder–1 tsp
- Broken cashewnuts– a handful
- Raisins (I didn't add them)–½ a cup
- Salt–pinch
- Ghee–2½ tbsp
- Baking Powder–1 tsp
- Grated coconut –1 cup (optional)
- Baking Soda–½ tsp

Method:

- Peel the cucumber, remove seeds and grate. Do not drain the water.

- Roast Semolina, in a pan with 1 tbsp ghee, on medium flame, till light brown.
- Add grated cucumber along with its water, jaggery, grated coconut and mix well.
- Cook the mixture without covering it till jaggery melts, keep stirring.
- Add chopped cashew nut, salt, cardamom powder and pure ghee and mix well.
- Prepare baking dish by applying pure ghee to the sides and bottom.
- Pre–heat the oven at 200 0 C for 10 minutes.
- Bake at 200 0 C for 30–35 minutes or till the upper crust is light brown.
- Cut into 1 x 1 inch pieces after cooling. Serve.

XXV
Dodha Burfi

Dhoda burfi's history is not that old and has been around since 1912. The dish originated in *Khushab*, Pakistan. Almost all the shops in and around the region claim it to be their own original recipe and the inventor of this dish and call it *Khushabi Dodha*. Dhoda burfi was invented as a form of energy food by Hans Raj, a local health conscious wrestler in Khushab. Conscious about his diet he wanted a food item which will be easy to carry around and yet provide energy and nutrients required during his wrestling sessions. He experimented and tried different combinations of high energy foods like wheat, milk, dry fruits. He then introduced this Dhoda fudge cake which was full of taste and served as an energy bar for him. Later, he commercialized the recipe and it was the invention of "*Dhoda*". After the Indo–Pak partition in 1947, his family moved to Kotkapura, Punjab, India and handed over the recipe to the local sweet makers in Khushab. Now, khushab is the land associated with the origin and pride of Dhoda.Dhoda is quite a simple dish and takes almost an hour to prepare. The ingredients needed to prepare Dhoda are milk, sugar, broken wheat, and clarified butter, dry fruits like pistachio, walnuts, cashew nuts and peanuts. It is often called as the close cousin of milk fudge; this desi treat is extensively prepared during winters and is slightly coarser than Peda.

Recipe:

Ingredients:

- Milk– 4 cup
- Heavy cream–1– ½ cup
- Sugar–2 cup

- Fine crack wheat (dahlia)–3 tbsp
- Clarified butter–1 tbsp
- Crushed cashews–1 cup
- Crushed almonds–1 cup
- Coco powder–2 tsp
- Sliced pistachios for garnishing–2 tbsp

Method:

- In a small pan stir fry crack wheat with butter over medium heat, till it turns brown in color. Set aside.
- In a heavy bottom pan over medium high heat boil the milk, and heavy cream, together.
- Let it boil till milk begins to thicken for about 40 minutes, stir occasionally and clean the sides to avoid the milk build up.
- Add crack wheat and sugar mix well and keep cooking for about 20 more minutes and stirring occasionally and clean the sides to avoid the milk build up.
- Add coco powder mix well, add cashews and almonds stir continuously till milk has become like soft dough and Burfi start leaving the sides of the pan and also Burfi has start leaving the butter. This should take about 15 minutes.
- Transfer the Dodha to 12 inch plate shaping it into square or rectangle in about ½ inch thick.
- While Dodha is still warm cut them in about one inch square. Sprinkle the pistachios over Dodha and lightly press them in.
- Dodha is ready to serve when it is at room temperature. Dhoda will stay good for about 2 weeks at room temperature or refrigerate for 2–3 months.

XXVI
Doodhpak

Doodhpak originates from Gujarat, a kind of rice pudding made from milk, rice, saffron and nuts. The milk is slow–boiled to thickened and sweetened and the dish is garnished with chopped almonds. It is known for its delectable flavours and textures. Doodh Paak is mostly prepared during the festive season in Gujarati and Parsi Household. This delicious and sinful Gujarati dessert is best served with Puri, Bhajiya (Pakora).

Recipe:

Ingredients:

- Milk– 1 liter
- Saffron Strands–a pinch
- Rice– 1 cup
- Sugar–1 cup
- Cardamom powder–½ tsp
- Chopped almonds–1 tbsp
- Ghee–1 tbsp
- Charoli–1 tbsp

Method:

- Wash the rice properly and drain it properly.
- Now, Add milk into a broad bottom pan and let it boil for 10 minutes, stirring occasionally.
- Then add ghee and rice to simmering milk and keep stirring.

- Let the rice cook for 10 minutes. When the rice becomes soft and thickens add sugar to it.
- Now, add cardamom powder, charoli and mix well and cook on medium heat for 10 minutes.
- Remove the pan from the heat.
- Garnish the Doodh pak with chopped almond and saffron strands and serve hot.

XXVII

Double ka Meetha

Double ka meetha or Bread ka Meetha is a bread pudding Indian sweet of fried bread slices soaked in hot milk with spices, including saffron and cardamom. Double ka meetha is a delicious dessert of Hyderabad, Telangana and is made at all most everyone's house. It is popular in Hyderabadi cuisine, served at weddings and parties. It is a traditional **N**izami dessert and served after having a heavy biryani. Double ka meetha refers to the maida loaf bread, called *"Double Roti"* in the local Indian dialects. The sweet, sugar and milk soaked fried pieces of bread with a lovely crunch from dry fruit in every bite. The dish is similar to *Shahi Tukra* which has its roots in Mughlai/Awadhi cuisine. It is particularly prepared during the festive month of Ramadan and on Eid. The recipe uses bread, condensed milk, and dry fruits.

Recipe:

Ingredients:

- Bread – 1 loaf
- Milk – 1 litre
- Khoa/mawa – 250 gms.
- Sugar – 500 gms.
- Almond – 100 gms.
- Cashew Nut – 100 gms.
- Pista – 100 gms.
- Raisins – 100 gms.
- Ghee – 250 gms.
- Cardamom – 10 gms.

- Water – 500 ml

Method:

- Trim the edges of the bread slices and cut each slice into four.
- Fry them in ghee till golden brown.
- Make sugar syrup by adding half a litre of water to the sugar. Add the milk to the sugar syrup. Boil till the syrup starts thickening.
- Powder the cardamom seeds.
- Add the powdered cardamom seeds and khoa/mawa to the thickened milk. Stir the mixture well.
- Arrange the fried bread pieces on a flat tray. Pour the syrup over the bread pieces while they are still hot. Garnish with the raisins and nuts.
- Refrigerate and serve.

XXVIII
Gajak

Gajak (also *gachak*) is a well–known dessert or confection originating from Morena in Madhya Pradesh. It is a dry sweet made of sesame seeds (til) or peanuts and jaggery. The til is cooked in the raw sugar syrup and set in thin layers, which can be stored for months.It is said that long time ago when India was ruled by the Mughal Emperors. They were non–vegetarians so they eat fish and meat to get strength, whereas king of Hindu Dynasty uses til, gur, chana for their soldiers to get energy, they used to feed their horses gur, chana for the energy during war. Therefore people at that time started using chana with gud, peanuts and til in order to get same level of energy. Later mixture of many material like til, gud, peanut, chana, dry fruit, kaju, badam ghee etc, become a part of sweet delicacy. This is how Gajak was introduced, with time it has changed but the originality is still the same. It is also believed that Sitaram Shivhare had invented the present form of crispy Gajak. In 1946, Chambal's pure water gave birth to crispy Gajak in Morena. When due to the dreaded dacoits of this region the people were frightened, at that time Sitaram Shivhare was busy in giving a new identity to this area. He wasbusy making a new sweet meat called Gajak by using jaggeryand til and pure water of Chambal. Making of Gajak is time consuming because it takes about 10–15 hours to prepare 5–8 kilograms. of Gajaks. The dough is hammered until all the sesame seeds break down and release their oils into the dough. Nowadays Gajaks are sold in various shapes like plain rectangular, rolled, balls, etc.

Recipe:

Ingredients:

- Sesame seeds–1 cup
- Soft, sticky jaggery–¾ cup
- Ghee–1 tbsp
- Oil for greasing pan–1 tsp
- Cardamom powder–¼ tsp

Method:

- Grease a pastry tray with oil, keep aside.
- Roast sesame seeds in a heavy pan, till they feel light and pinkish.
- Remove, keep aside.
- Melt jaggery over low heat, in a large heavy pan.
- Add Ghee, cardamom, stir gently till smooth.
- Add sesame seeds, mix gently.
- Pour into tray, allow to cool till warm.
- Mark out indentations for squares as desired.
- Allow to cool completely, before storing in airtight containers.

XXIX
Gavvalu

Sweet shells are one of the typical Indian sweets made in Andhra Pradesh, India. It is a mixture (dough) of plain flour/maida and water or milk. The prepared dough is shaped into small rounds, which are flattened and rolled (on a special tool) so as to take the shape of gavvalu (cowrie shells). These shells are fried in oil or ghee and are poured into sugar or jaggery syrup. This sweet is basically prepared in every household in Andhra Pradesh during Janmashtmi and during Laxmi Puja in Deepawali. Gavvalu are small shells found in the sea and is believed to be precious as it resemble coins during barter system of business in the earlier times. According to legend Laxmi is believed to be the daughter of sea, hence it is thus believed that wherever there are shells (cowrie), there is Laxmi or wealth. Gavvalu is prepared by special serrated wooden tool known as *"Gavvala Peeta"*. These are similar to *or Kulkuls* prepared during the Christmas celebrations in Goa.

Kidyoor Kulkula –is a Goan special Christmas sweet recipe. Traditionally these are specially prepared by the Catholics in Goa and are distributed to neighbors, friends and relatives during Christmas. These are fried cookies resembling sea shells.

Recipe:

Ingredients:

- Ghee – 2 tbsp
- Maida – 2 cup
- Oil – to fry
- Salt – 1 pinch
- Sugar – 1cup

- Water – 2tbsp

Method:

- Take a bowl pour maida into it add ghee and mix well.
- Now add water to make dough, the dough should not be too hard or soft.
- Take a Fork turn back side, then take a small piece of dough into hand and press at the back side of the fork and remove opposite direction repeat the same way for all the dough. Keep the shells a side.
- Now take a pan add oil for fry add the shells into the oil and deep fry till light golden brown colour fry in a low flame.
- Once it is done remove from oil and keep it a side.
- Now take another pan add sugar and little water and let it boil till you get a thick consistency and remove from the flame.
- Add the fried shells to the sugar syrup once the sugar sticks to shells transfer these shells into another plate

XXX

Ghari

Ghari or Surti Ghari is a sweet Gujarati dish from Surat, Gujarat. Ghari is made of puri batter, mawa, ghee and sugar. It is also available in many varieties and flavours such as pistachio, almond–elachi and mawa. It is generally made on *Chandani Padva* festival. There is a history behind Ghari. Priest Nirmaladasji referred Devshankar Shukla to make Ghari in 1838. Ghari was also prepared by the Devshankar Shukla for Tatya Tope to provide extra strength to the freedom fighter's soldiers in 1857 on a full moon day which is now celebrated as Chandi padwa. However, it began to be consumed during inauspicious occasions too, particularly by people of some castes in the crematorium for peace to the soul of the dead. Chandi Padwa is one of very popular festival of Surti people. Huge amount of gharis gets made in Surat during Chandi Padwa which is a big business.It helps many small and big vendors to make decent amount of money during this festival time! Ghari stuffing can be anything sweet, mostly it's filled with either semolina, mawa & nuts and the covering is maida bread.

Recipe:

Ingredients:

For the layer–

- Maida – 1 cup
- Melted ghee – 2 tbsp
- About – ¼ cup
- Milk – as per req.

For the filling–

- Crushed pistachio – 1 cup
- Crushed badam – 1 cup
- Mava or khoya – 2 cups
- Rava – 1 tbsp
- Besan – 2 tbsp
- Cardamom powder – 1 tsp
- Saffron – a pinch soaked in 1 tsp milk
- Sugar – 3/4 cup or as req.

To Fry–

- 1½ cup oil + ¼ cup ghee (Only oil or ghee can be used)

For glaze–

- Ghee – 1/3 cup (about 6 tbsp)
- Powder sugar – 3/4 cup

Method:
Preparing the Dough–

- Make soft dough with maida, ghee and milk. Leave it for 20 mins.

Preparing the Stuffing–

- Fry besan and rava in ghee for 3 mins. Add mava or khoya (or cream and milk powder) and cook for 4–5 mins. Take out the mixture into the plate to cool faster.
- When cooled completely, add cardamom powder, sugar and mix everything. Divide it into 2 portions.
- Add crushed almond, saffron and to one portion and add crushed pista and to other portion. Use little milk at a time to bind the both mixture.
- Make small balls of each. Flatten the almond ball in between your palm. Keep pista ball in the centre and cover it nicely.

Preparing Ghari–

- Roll out to thin puris of 4‖ diameter. Place 1 ball in each puri and cover it nicely . cut off the extra dough portion and deep fry in ghee on low flame. Let it cool down for 4 hours.
- For garnishing–
- Melt ghee slightly and add sugar and whip it lightly. Dip each ghari in the ghee and set aside for 12 hours to become firm. Garnish it with pista. Cut each ghari into 4 pieces and serve.

XXXI
Ghevar

Ghevar is a disc–shaped Indian sweet having a crispy but porous texture. It is prepared using maida and ghee,mildly fried in moulds, soaked in sugar syrup and dressed with rabri or dry fruits. It is a traditional sweet dish of Rajasthan and western Uttar Pradesh and mostly prepared and served during the Teej and Rakshbandhan festivals.As per ayurveda, the months of Shravan and Bhadrapada i.e. July–August–September are predominated with *Vata* and *Pitta* respectively. This causes dryness and acidity in the whole body, resulting in restlessness and mood swings. The highly sweet and ghee laden Ghevar provide relief from the acidic and moist environment. They have Vata and Pitta calming properties due to ghee and sweet juice. Thus, they have a calming effect on mind as well as the body. Furthermore, ghevar is a carrier of love, care and blessings of parents to their married daughters. Ritually the ghever is core item among gifts sent to daughters on this day with blessing for a blissful married life. The month of *sawan* is allied with Lord Shiva and his union with Parvati, as they are considered the eternal cosmic pair, parents do bless their daughters for the same. Ghevars are available in many colours and varieties including plain, mawa, malai and are very colourful.

Recipe:

Ingredients:

- Maida –500 gms
- Ghee– 150 gms
- Water –1.5 litre
- Milk– 1 litre

- Sugar– 50 gms
- Cardamom powder– 5 gms
- Saffron– 1 gram
- Chopped fried nuts– 50 gms

For sugar syrup–

- Sugar– 500 gms
- Water– 250 ml
- Saffron– a pinch
- Ghee– (for frying)

Method:

- Heat Ghee in a heavy bottom pan and cool by adding ice, by this all the impurities are left behind and pure ghee gets accumulated on the surface.
- Massage the ghee nicely till it is smooth and start incorporating the flour and water slowly till you get batter.
- Heat ghee in a heavy bottom pan,place a circular mold and start pouring the batter in center, fry till it is golden brown.
- Make sugar syrup by heating water and sugar till the sugar dissolves completely.
- Add the fried Ghevar to the warm syrup and remove.
- To make malai heat milk, sugar,cardamom powder and saffron and reduce to half,cool till it thickens.
- Top the malai on the ghevar and garnish with chopped nuts.

XXXII

Gujiya

Call it a cousin of Turkish Baklava, a co–traveller of *Sambusa* (now famous as samosa) from Arabia or the result of the culinary exploits of the last Mughals, who had lost the whole of India but their love for food and revelry, the desi Gujiya‘s journey has been quite a fascinating one. These crunchy flour pastries, filled with sweet fillings have formed a part of several rituals and celebrations through the ages. The exact date of Gujiya‘s association with *Holi* is not known, but it has been a part of the celebratory kitchen of the courtiers of the Mughals and the Nawabs since a few hundred years. Gujias are prepared in Uttar Pradesh, Rajasthan, Gujrat and Bihar regions of India, and in Nepal, Bangladesh, during Holi and Diwali festivities. They are called *Purukiya* in Bihar. Purukiyas are very popular in Bihar and are relished by everyone. There are two types of purukiya made in Bihar– one with suji / rawa (Semolina) and another with khoya. In suji purukiya, suji is roasted in ghee with sugar, cashew, grated coconut, cardamom, raisins and other nuts and then deep fried in ghee. In khoya purukiya, pure khoya is mixed with nuts and sugar and then deep fried. It is also called *Ghughra* (Gujarati) in Gujarat, *Karanji* (Marathi) in Maharashtra, *Somas* (Tamil) in Tamil Nadu, *Garijalu* (Telugu) in Telangana and, *Kajjikaya or Kajjikayalu* (Telugu/Kannada) in Andhra Pradesh and Karnataka. They are all fried sweet dumplings made of wheat flour and stuffed with dry or moist coconut delicacies. In Goa, Goans prepare a similar sweet on the occasion of their festivals– Hindus for Ganesh Chaturthi and Christians for Christmas, and call it *Nevri* or *Neuri* (plural Neureo). In Odisha it is called —*Karanji*‖ and has either a coconut based or chhena based filling.Traditionally a sweet offered to friends and relatives during the festival of colours, Gujiya can be made in a number of ways and here is a list of some popular variations found across India–

Perukiya– Made in Bihar and Jharkhand, this Gujiya variety has a mixture of semolina and mawa as filling (together or separately) and is deep–fried but not put in sugar syrup. It has an unmistakable crunch and is not too high on sugar.

Somas–Somas or Karchikai or Somasi is a traditional sweet prepared for Diwali in Tamil Nadu. The sweet filling is usually made with Bengal gram powder, rava and sugar and khoya.

Karanji–In Karanji, the stuffing includes dry fruits like cashew, almond and raisins and also has lots of fresh coconut along with cardamom powder and nutmeg. The Karanjis are deep–fried and can be stored in air–tight containers for longer periods.

Ghughra– Called Ghughra in Gujarat, gujiya of this type is made by making a mixture of rava, coconut, sugar and dry fruits which is then stuffed in flour pastries and deep– fried.

Nevri– Prepared by Goan Hindus on the occasion of Ganesh Chaturthi, this variation of Gujiya has coconut, sugar, poppy seeds and cardamom powder.

Kajjikaya– Popular in Andhra Pradesh and Karnataka, this variety has dry or moist coconut as stuffing along with dry fruits.

Recipe of simple Gujiya:

Ingredients:

For the dough –

- refined flour– 2 cups
- clarified butter– 1 cup
- Water– (to mix)

For the filling -

- Khoya–1 cup
- Sugar–1 cup
- green cardamom, powdered–1 tsp
- chironji–1 tbsp
- Ghee (for deep–frying)

For the syrup (Optional) =

- Sugar–1 cup
- Water–1 cup

Method:

Prepare the dough–

- Rub ¼ cup ghee into the flour and knead into stiff dough with water.
- Leave to rest for at least half an hour.

Prepare the filling–

- Sauté the khoya over medium heat till it looks slightly fried.
- Take off the heat and when it cools, mix in the sugar, cardamom and almonds.
- Shape the filling into ovals about 21 cm length and 1 cm thickness.
- Make balls of the dough and roll out into 1 cm / 1/8 in thick rounds.
- Take a round, wet the edges with water and place a piece of filling over one half.
- Fold the other half over and press the edges together to seal.
- Either cut off the edge with a fancy cutter or make a design by pinching and twisting all along the sealed edges.
- Make all the gujiyas in this way. Heat ghee in a kadahi. To check if the ghee is hot enough put a piece of dough in it. If it comes up at once, add as many gujiyas as fit in comfortably.
- Turn them over and lower the heat to medium. Fry till golden brown on all sides. Lift out and leave to drain on absorbent paper.
- Make sugar syrup by cooking water and sugar together, till one thread consistency. Dipping into sugar syrup is optional. Gujiyas can be eaten dry.
- Dip the gujiyas in it, lift and let dry on a plate.
- Fry the rest, increasing the heat for a few seconds before adding the next lot.
- Can be eaten hot or at room temperature and can be stored in air–tight containers.

XXXIII

Gulab Jamun

Gulab jamun is a dessert that dates back to medieval India. It is a milk–solid–based sweet made mainly from khoya and dipped in sugar syrup. It is often garnished with dried nuts such as almonds to enhance flavour. It is said to have originated from Persia, and rose to popularity in the Mughal era when it was consumed by the sultans who got it to our land.

The original name for the much–loved dessert is *Luqmat Al– Qadi*. It is derived from a fritter that Persian speaking invaders brought to India. The etymology of 'gulab jamun' is derived from the roots *gol* (flower), *ab* (water) and *jamun* (a round Indian fruit). This is because the dish is essentially composed of round pieces of mawa and flour immersed in saffron flavored syrup. Legend says that Gulab Jamun was first prepared by the *Chef of Shahjahan*, the Mughal king famous for creating Taj Mahal, one of the Seven Wonders of the World. He is said to have been inspired by the Persian desert and soon, this was popularized among us as a royal dessert.

Gulab Jamun is always the perfect dessert idea for wedding reception, a casual dinner party, a birthday celebration or even mourning or any other festival. Gulab Jamuns go with every mood and occasion. While some, including me, prefer it boiling hot, with minimum syrup and to savor every bite, some prefer it with cold kulfi/ vanilla ice cream, the sweet hot and cold combination confusing and pleasing their senses.

Variations of Gulab Jamun:

Ledikeni–As per the most famous story, in the late 1850s, Calcutta's expert confectioner Bhim Chandra Nag was approached to set up a unique sweet for Lady Canning – the spouse of Governor General Lord Charles Canning (later the primary Viceroy of British India) – who was coming to

India to be with her better half. This unusual dessert caught the aristocratic Lady Canning's attention and because of her fondness of the dessert.By the act of God, or a genius or perhaps a mistake the sweet he prepared began to be called by the locals as Ledikeni, which was more of a mispronunciation of her name. Lady Canning served this delicate dessert in all her parties and gathering. It is also said that she is likely to popularize the dessert all over Bengal.

Pantua– a smaller version of Gulab jamun which is stuffed with sugar balls or mishri or nuts.

Kalajam or Kala jamun – This variant of Gulab Jamun has a purple–black color as opposed to the traditional golden–brown color. It is sweeter as there is an addition of sugar to the batter before deep frying it at a high temperature.

Jhurre Ka Rasgulla– many times bigger than usual gulab jamun, prepared in local desi ghee and sold in Katangi, in Jabalpur

Lyancha– elongated or cylindrical shaped gulab jamun sold in various sweet shops in Kolkata.

Recipe:

Ingredients:

- Maida–½ cup
- Mawa–200–225 gms
- Baking Soda– 1/8 tsp
- Ghee (or oil)– for deep frying
- Cardamom Powder–¼ + ¼ tsp
- Saffron Strands –8–10
- Sugar–1½ cups
- Milk–1 tsp
- Water–2½ cups

Method:

- With the heel of your palm or the base of a flat metal bowl, mash the khoya, so that no grains remain.
- Mix in the flour baking soda and ¼ tsp. cardamom powder and knead into firm dough. You can use a food processor too.
- The dough should be firm but pliable and should not feel dry. If it does feel dry, wet your hands and work the dough again.

- Shape the dough into marble–sized balls (jamuns) that are smooth and creaseless. The shape can be round or oblong.
- Heat ghee in the kadahi till a piece of dough tossed in comes up at once.
- Lower heat and fry a cube of bread till light brown (this lowers the temperature of the ghee).
- Lift out bread and add as many jamuns as will fit in, without one touching the other.
- Keeping the heat low, fry these till a golden brown all over.
- Drain the jamuns out of the ghee, and fry the next lot, increasing the heat for a few seconds and then lowering it again before adding the jamuns.
- Keep the gulab jamuns aside till the syrup is ready.
- Mix the sugar and water and place over low heat, stirring till the sugar dissolves. Make sure it does not boil.
- Increase the heat once the sugar dissolves, and then bring mixture to a boil.
- Add the milk and water mixture and continue boiling over high flame, without stirring.
- Skim off any scum that collects on the sides of the pan.
- Cook till syrup thickens a bit. A finger dipped in slightly cold syrup should form a coating on it for a few seconds.
- Take syrup off stove and cool for a minimum of half an hour. Strain through a fine nylon sieve or muslin cloth.
- Add cardamom and bring syrup to a boil again.
- Add the fried gulab jamuns to it and put off the heat. Let jamuns soak for at least half an hour before serving.

Halbai

It is one of the popular traditional delicacies from the dupe and Mangalore cuisine and is generally made for occasions and celebration feast such as Nagarpanchmi. It is very simple and easy to make as it contains very basic ingredients like rice, jaggery and coconut. It tastes very good when consumed with ghee. The color of the Halbai is totally depends on the Jaggery which is used.

Recipe:

Ingredients:

- White Rice – 1 cup
- Jaggery – 1 cup
- Grated Coconut – 3/4 cup
- Cardamom – 2
- Salt – a pinch
- Ghee or clarified butter – 2 tsp

Method:

- Wash and soak rice in water for about 4 to 5 hours.
- In a mixer jar, take soaked rice, grated coconut, and cardamom with half cup of water added to it. Grind all these ingredients until the whole mixture turns into smooth paste.
- Grease a plate with plain surface (like a big stainless steel plate) with ½ tsp of ghee. Keep aside.

- In a vessel, add 1 and 1/2 cup water, salt and ghee. When the water boils, add 1 cup of Jaggery to the vessel. Boil the Water until the Jaggery dissolves completely. Sometimes you may find sugarcane bits in jaggery; if so, try to filter the jaggery water with the help of strainer. Once the jaggery water is filtered, transfer it back to the vessel and boil for a minute and reduce the flame to low.
- Now add the rice – coconut paste from Step 2 above to the boiling jaggery water, keep stirring the mixture until the whole sticky mass starts leaving the sides of the vessel. Ensure that no lumps are formed by continuously stirring the contents of the vessel.
- Remove from the fire and then pour the Halbai paste to the Ghee greased plate and spread evenly. Leave it to cool.
- Once cooled, cut the Halbai to your favorite shape and size. Halbai or Rice Halwa is now ready to serve.

Halwa

Halwa refers to dense, gelatinous sweet confection that is very popular in India, Pakistan and many Asian countries, European countries and Jewish world. Halwa is also available as crumby form made from nuts and stiff square varieties like the ice halwa found in India. The word halwa is actually Arabic and it derived from the word "*hilwa*" which means 'sweet' and in Arabic, it is pronounced as "*hullwaa*" and is served with tea or coffee. It is delicious, wonderful and healthy sweet.

The first known written halvah recipe appeared in the early 13th century Arabic Kitab al–Tabikh (The Book of Dishes). According to Alan Davidson of The Oxford Companion to Food, halwa is an Arabic dish. Halwa may also be based on various other ingredients, including beans, lentils, and vegetables such as carrots, pumpkins, yams and squashes.

Food historians hint that the halwa is as old as the hills and has its roots sometime in 3000 B.C.E., while many others hold the opinion that mentions of a gummy, greasy, sweet confection can be found even in early references (12th century) of Istanbul. Be that as it may, the word halava is thought to be Arabic and finds its origins in the word halwa, meaning sweet dish or sweetmeat. But then, the Halwa had quite a journey as mentioned before, which is why it was rechristened as halava in Sanskrit, *Sajjige* in Kannada, *Halawa* in Egypt, *Makedonikos* Halvas in Greece, *halvah* in Hebrew, *hilwa* or *halawi* in Arabic, *helva* in Turkey and *halva* back here in India.

In northern India, the most famous include sooji (or suji) halwa (semolina), aate ka halwa (wheat), moong dal ka halwa, gajar halwa (carrot) which traditionally belongs to Punjab and is referred to as gajrela, dudhi halwa, chana daal halwa (chickpeas), and Kaju halwa (cashew nut).

Kashi halwa– made from winter melon or ash gourd, is a famous and traditional sweet of Karnataka, and mainly makes a regular appearance in traditional Brahmin weddings. Tirunelveli in Tamil Nadu is known for its wheat halwa.*Aate ka Halwa* usually being served every day as prasad after reciting hymns in Sikh Gurudwaras.

Mahim halwa– is an Indian sweet translated as *"layered semolina sweet"*, named after Mahim an area in Mumbai. This flat, palm sized melt–in–the–mouth goodness invented by a family of sweetmeat and snacks makers who migrated from Jamnagar, now in Gujarat. It is named so because it was created by the sweet meat makers *"Joshi Budha kaka"*(Buddha kaka means–old uncle) who belong to Mahim. It has been described as a "unique confection of thin layers of sweet dough pressed into compact squares and separated by sheets of greaseproof paper.

Satyanarayan halwa – variation of suji halwa, with the addition of detectable traces of banana.

Recipe of Gajar ka halwa:

Ingredients:

- Carrots–1 kg
- Milk–1 litre
- Cardamom seeds–1 tsp
- Water–3/4 cup
- Ghee–3 tbsps
- Mawa–100 gms
- Raisins–2 tbsps
- Almonds–2 tbsps
- Pistachios–2 tbsps
- Sugar–450 gms.

Method:

- Wash and grate the carrots. Soak the raisins in water for 30 minutes. Blanch and shred the nuts.
- Put the water to boil, when it starts boiling add the grated carrots. Cook for 5– 7 minutes.
- Add the milk. Cook on a low flame for 1 hour stirring occasionally. Add sugar, mix well and cook till the sugar has dissolved and all the milk has been absorbed.

- Add half of the mawa and mix well.
- Add ghee and simmer for 2–3 minutes. Add the slightly crushed cardamoms and the raisins. Mix well.
- Remove the gajar halwa from heat and arrange in a serving dish. Garnish with the rest of mawa, almonds and pistachios.
- Serve cold, hot or at room temperature.

XXXVI
Imarti

Imarti, which is also known as *mriti*, *Emarti*, *Omriti*, *Jahangir* and *Jhangiri/ Jaangiri*, is a Rajasthani dessert of Persian origin. It was once considered a royal confectionery and served in the courts of the Rajputs and the Mughals in India. It is red–orange in color, shaped somewhat like a circular pretzel, and has a chewy, sugary texture. Imarti is related to another confectionery known as jalebi, which also has Persian roots and is very popular in the Indian subcontinent; This sweet dish originated in India in the Mughal kitchens in Fatehpur Sikri. Many sweet shops in India, particularly those in the northern parts, sell imartis and jalebis. These desserts are made on festive occasions and are also eaten as a warming food in the winter, usually with buttermilk. Beniram ki Imarti is one of the oldest Imarti shop in Jaunpur (UP). It is almost 200 years old.

Imarti ingredients are urad dal, rice, sugar, water, saffron color, rose essence, cardamon and ghee. The urad dal and rice are soaked overnight in water. The following day the water is drained away and the soaked dal and rice mixture is ground.

Recipe:

Ingredients:

- Dhuli urad dal (husked Bengal Gram – soaked in water overnight) – 2 cups
- Sugar – 3 cups
- Water1 – ½ cup
- Saffron color – few strands
- Cardamom ground – ½ tsp

- Ghee (to fry) – 500 gram

Method:

- Wash, drain and grind the daal with minimum water (should be thick). Mix in the colour.
- Beat daal well till fluffy, a drop dropped in water should float.
- Keep aside fermenting for 3 – 4 hours in Summer, more in Winter.
- Dissolve sugar in the water over low heat, stirring continuously till sugar is dissolved (do not let it come to a boil before that).
- Cook till one thread consistency (a drop pressed between fingers and pulled apart, should form a thin thread).
- Add cardamom powder. Pipe the batter with a nozzle or cloth with a hole, to form imartis straight into the hot ghee.
- Lower flame and allow crisping turning once.
- Remove from ghee, drop into the hot syrup for 3 – 4 minutes, drain and serve.

XXXVII
Jalebi

A traditionally festive sweet, jalebi, is the popular dessert of any Indian palate and is available in every mithai shop. Jalebis vary in thickness, size, colour and weight. The name itself is a corruption of the *zalabiya* (Arab) or *zoolabiya* (Persian) and versions of it are found all over the Middle East. In Afghanistan, jalebis are traditionally served with fish in the winter. In Iran, it is a festive dish, and also served to the poor during Ramadan.

The origins of jalebi have been traced back to ancient India, where it was called *Kundalika* or *Jal–vallika*. It is said that this name was given because the sweet was full of watery syrup. *Jal–vallika* then became Jalebi in later dialects, sometime during the period of Muslim rule, by means of trade and cultural exchanges with the Indian subcontinent. And soon enough, Jalebi became Zalebi as 'J' sound was non– existent in middle–eastern languages and 'Z' was the closest equivalent sound. While the jalebi obviously traveled through the old trade routes to make its way across the region, there are many variations to it, with ingredients that vary as well. For example in some parts of the country, the batter used to make jalebi consists of urad dal and rice flour with a little besan or ground gram and wheat flour. In some other parts, it also includes semolina and baking powder. In Bengal, dairy products like chhena and khoa are added to the jalebi.

Jalebis are prepared in different types like:

Chhena jalebi–Chhena Jalebi or Paneer jalebi is a sweet dish originally from coastal Odisha in eastern India, a state known for desserts made of chhena. Its popularity has spread beyond coastal Odisha to Bengal. However, the basic ingredient is fresh curd cheese called chenna. Fresh chhena is thoroughly kneaded and rolled up into shapes similar to pretzels, before being deep fried It is more browner than common jalebi. Chhena jilapis are served either hot or chilled.

Jaleba–Jaleba is bigger than Jalebi, It typically weighs 250 gms. or more, but can be prepared up to 500 gms. as well and is often fried in pure desi ghee. It is served hot off the girdle, after being soaked in saffron–flavoured sugar syrup. It is very popular in Western Madhya Pradesh, especially Indore.

Jhangiri– Jhangiri/Jangri is Jalebi's cousin who settled in South India. A famous sweet southwards of the Vindhyas, it appears similar to the jalebi but has its own very distinct personality. The difference comes from the way Jangiri is prepared. It is made with ground urad dal which makes it a healthier but lighter. A good Jangiri is a lot more soft and chewy as compared to jalebi. According to legends prince Salim aka Jehangir was bored having the same sweet every day, so he ordered his *khansamas* to prepare something new urgently. The khansama did not much time for preparation; instead he took the raw batter of urad dal, mixed with a bit of maida and made a bit bigger jalebis. This recipe was very much liked by the Sultan as it was transparent, less sweeter, crunchy and light. Thus originated the famous Jhangri from the Mughal kitchen.

Imarti– Imarti or Omriti, is another of Jalebi's cousins, and is mostly found in the north. Thicker and juicier than its cousin, Imarti has a very prominent flower–like shape and a distinct preparation method. It is made using urad dal, cornflour and saffron and then dipped into flavorfully prepared sweet sugar syrup with green cardamom powder; imarti is traditionally best served cold.

Khoya jalebi –A specialty of Jabalpur, Madhya Pradesh, khoya or mawa jalebi is made using a batter of khoya, thickened evaporated milk commonly used to make Indian desserts, and milk with a little maida, which acts as a binding agent. While this jalebi can be enjoyed on its own, it tastes even better when topped with cold milk or malai.

Recipe of simple Jalebi:

Ingredients:

- Refined flour (maida) – 1 cup
- Yogurt – ½ cup
- Sugar – 3 cups
- Milk – 1 tbsp
- Saffron (kesar) – a few

- Ghee for deep–frying

Method:

- In a large bowl, whisk refined flour, yogurt and sufficient water to a smooth and pouring consistency batter. Cover and keep in a warm place to ferment for 24 hours.
- Beat the batter with your hands again for 15 minutes. Cook sugar with 2 cups water in a deep non–stick pan on high heat, stirring continuously, till the sugar dissolves.
- Add milk and when the scum rises to the top, collect it with a ladle and discard.
- Add saffron and cook, stirring, till the syrup reaches one string consistency. Keep the syrup warm. Heat sufficient ghee in a kadai on medium heat.
- Pour some batter onto a jalebi cloth, gather the edges and make a tight potli.
- Squeeze round spirals into the hot ghee and deep fry, turning them over gently a few times, till they are evenly golden and crisp.
- Drain and soak in sugar syrup for 2–3 minutes. Take them out of the syrup and serve hot.

XXXVIII
Kaju Katli

Kaju katli (literally "cashew slices"), also known as Kaju barfi, is an Indian dessert similar to a barfi. Kaju means cashew; Barfi is often, but not always, made by thickening milk with sugar and other ingredients (such as dry fruits and mild spices).

These days, kaju katlis are made in all parts of India. However, its origin is in the western territories of the country. As the story goes, Kaju katli was created during the reign of Jehangir. He had captivated several Sikh gurus and kings and held them for many years in the Gwalior fort. The condition of living was palpable and the prisoners were in constant suffering. One of the prisoners was the 6th Sikh Guru, *Guru Hargovind* himself. He helped in making the prisoners self-sufficient inside the fort and improved the quality of life of all inmates and guards with his teachings. Emperor Jahangir declared that the Guru is to be released and anyone who can cling on to his robe while he walks out will be free too. Guru Hargovind secretly set the 52 kings to create a robe long enough for everyone in the prison to hold on to. And all prisoners walked scott free holding on to the long robe on the day of Diwali. Sikhs all over celebrate this day of liberation as *Bandhi Chor diwas.* On that day of liberation Jahangir's royal chef had prepared the kaju barfi for the first time as a token of appreciation for the Sikh guru. The Kaju barfi was originally made with thickened milk or rabri mixed with ground cashews and almonds.

Nowadays Kaju katli is one of the most popular Indian sweets and probably the most gifted sweet in by any elite class in any occasion and celebration.

Recipe:

Ingredients:

- Cashews–1 cup
- Sugar–½ cup
- Water–¼ cup
- Gr.cardamom powder – 1/8 tsp
- Ghee –1 tsp
- Silver vark – optional
- Saffron – optional

Method:

- Firstly, in a small mixer jar, take 1 cup cashews.
- Furthermore, grind to smooth powder. Keep aside.
- Now in a nonstick pan, take ½ cup of sugar along with ¼ cup of water.
- Keep the flame on low and keep on stirring to form syrup.
- Stir the sugar syrup till it forms 1 string consistency.
- Now sieve the ground cashew powder.
- Remember to keep the flame on low all the time and give a good mix.
- Add cardamom / saffron and continue to mix till it starts releasing from pan.
- Once the cashew paste turns to dough leaving the pan add a tsp of ghee.
- Continue to mix till the ghee melts completely and cashew dough is formed leaving the pan.
- Switch off the stove. And grease the butter paper with ghee.
- Transfer the cashew dough on to the butter paper.
- Grease your hand with little ghee and knead 30 seconds.
- Once you get smooth dough, cover with butter paper.
- Take a plate and press to form uniform layer.
- Then roll the dough with a rolling–pin, adjusting the thickness according to your choice.
- Cut the edges so that you can get perfect diamond shapes.
- Now cut the dough into diamond shape or the shape you wish for.
- You can also decorate with silver leaf / silver vark and serve.

XXXIX
Kaju and Pista Roll

Kaju or cashew nut is a rich ingredient used in both sweet and savoury dishes all around the world. With the festive season right around the corner, we have the most popular kaju sweet for you, the kaju pista roll. Prepare this for a dinner party and serve your guests these delicious, sweet little rolls, filled with dry fruits and garnished with silver leaf.

Recipe:

Ingredients :

- Cashew nuts – 2 cup
- Icing Sugar/powdered sugar – 1 cup
- Pistachios – 1.5 cup
- Condensed milk – 1 cup
- Desi ghee / clarified butter – 2 tbsp
- Cardamom powder – 1/2 tsp
- Green colour – 1/2 tsp
- Kewra essence – 4 drops
- Silver vark – 3 sheets(optional)

Method:

- First of all, grind the cashews and pistachios separately in a dry mixer for 1 minute. Sieve the powder to get rid of any big chunk left behind.
- Place a nonstick pan over medium flame and add 1.5 tablespoon desi ghee or clarified butter. Once it melts add condensed milk. Stir continuously for 30 seconds to combine together.

- Add cashew nut powder. Cook the mixture on slow heat; keep stirring for 3 – 4 minutes until the mixture starts to leave edges of pans and forms into dough.
- Once mixture comes together turn off flame and keep stirring for a minute, allowing it to cool. Once its luke warm, take it out in a plate and add 1/4 tablespoon of clarified butter to it. Start kneading it well to make smooth dough.
- Now take pistachios powder in a large mixing bowl and add icing sugar/ powdered sugar. Add green food colour and 1/4 tablespoon clarified butter to it and mix well to form dough with the help of few water drops.
- Now both cashew nut dough and pistachios dough are ready. Divide the cashew dough and pistachios dough into 4 portions. Take a butter paper and grease some butter on it. Place one portion of cashew dough on it and cover it with another piece of greased butter paper. Roll the cashew dough into thin circle of 4 inch diameter with the help of a rolling pin.
- Now shape one portion of pista dough into a stick and place them over the cashew sheet. Start rolling them and pinch the edges. Smooth the roll and cut roll into 4 pieces.
- Repeat same process for rest of the 3 portions. Garnish them with silver vark.

XL
Kalakand

Kalakand, or Qalaqand is a popular Indian sweet made out of solidified, sweetened milk and cottage cheese. It owes it origin to the milk–rich Braj area of western Uttar Pradesh. It is a very popular sweetmeat in North and East India, including Jharkhand, Orissa and Bengal and is reputed for its exquisite taste. The term qand in qalaqand is derived from the Arabic language and means sweets.

Baba Thakur Dasji came to India from Pakistan, after the Partition. He was a halwai (sweet maker) in Dera Ismail Khan Gaon in Pakistan and when he reached India, he relocated himself in Alwar and started selling this sweet meat. Call it Alwar Kalakand, Alwar ka Mawa or Alwar ka Milk cake and it tastes just as delicious. Baba Thakur Das & Sons, located on Hope Circus at the Kalakand Market. In Western India, its fried version or the Ajmeri Kalakand is more in demand, where it is also known as milk cake. The best part of Ajmeri Kalakand is that it is fried with lots of fresh figs (hence Anjeer Kalakand), which imparts a grainy texture to it and enhance the flavour too. One more famous kalakand comes from Jhumri Telaiya in Bihar. According to the records, in the late 50s, "Bhati Brothers from Pakistan came to Jhumri Telaiya after partition" and started selling the creamy version of "Kalakand". With the passage of time, the demand of Kalakand soared high which made Jhumri Telaiya a gastronomical destination for people.

Recipe:

Ingredients:

- Milk – 1.5 kg

- Sugar – 100gms
- Kesar (saffron) – few strands
- Vinegar – 2 tbsp
- Dry fruits – for garnish

Method:

- Boil the milk in a saucepan, adding sugar and kesar.
- When it reduces to almost half, set aside 150 ml of the sweetened milk.
- Now add vinegar to the boiling milk and stir it slowly for a few minutes.
- Cover the saucepan and let the mixture rest for 15 minutes.
- When the milk and whey separate completely, drain out the whey and slightly mash the cottage cheese using your hands (don't use a mixer–grinder).
- In a separate pan, heat 100 ml of the sweetened saffron milk that you had set aside and add the cottage cheese to it.
- When the milk dries up and the mixture thickens (here, you can add some milk powder, though it's optional), turn off the heat.
- Now spread the milk mixture on a greased tray and level the surface.
- Leave it for an hour or more.
- Once cool and set, pour the remaining 50 ml of the sweetened milk on top of it and garnish with dry fruits. Cut into squares and serve.

XLI

Kanchagola

This authentic sweetmeat, originating in eastern India, is considered the purest form of sweet to be offered to the Goddess. Known as kaccha gola or kacha golla, the taste of this sweet is blissful. Each ball is so soft that it will melt in your mouth in a fraction of seconds. Legend has it that *Queen Bhabani* of Natore had one *Modhusudan Das* of the nearby Lalbajar region supply her with sweets. Modhusudan once had a bit of trouble with an absentee employee and about 80 kilograms of chhana (is fresh, unripened curd cheese made from milk) sitting in his shop, intended for supply to the queen. So, while trying to figure out how to save the chhana from going bad, he added some syrup, and kept stirring, only to see the syrup evaporate. To see how the chhana fared, he tasted it, and found it quite delicious. The queen loved that too and it became a regular feature on her table. During Rani Bhabani's time, the reputation of the famous Kacha Golla spread abroad. Even today, 250 years ago, despite its invention, its reputation abroad still remains. This dish features regularly in Bengali wedding, Navratri and Dussera festivals.

Recipe:

Ingredients:

- Fresh, fullcream milk – 2 litres
- Lemon juice or vinegar – 4 tbsp
- Saffron strands – 8–10
- Green cardamom powder – ¼ tsp
- Granulated sugar (amount can be varied according to individual preference) – 5 tbsp

- Fine muslin or cheesecloth
- Water – 5 tbsp

Method:

- Pour 1 tbsp water in a wok or a kadhai (so that the milk doesn't stick to the bottom of the wok) and add the milk. Bring it to boil, adding the saffron strands stirring from time to time. Slowly add 4 tbsp lemon juice mixed with equal amount of water, till the cheese and the whey just start to separate. Switch off the gas immediately to prevent hardening of the cheese.
- After around 3 min, pour the chenna (the cottage cheese) and the whey into cheesecloth or a muslin cloth and run cold water on this to arrest further curdling and to wash away the lemony smell.
- Tie the cloth and squeeze the extra whey. Keep this cloth on a perforated plate or a flat colander. Put a heavy, flat object on this for 20 min, so that there is no extra whey left in the cottage cheese.
- After 20 min, open the cloth and remove the saffron – infused cheese on another flat surface. Mash the cheese thoroughly for around 15 min with your palm. Finally, a stage would be reached when there are no lumps in the chenna and it can be turned into a smooth and creamy ball.
- Break the ball once again and add the cardamom powder and the sugar. Knead well once again. The process will take five to seven more minutes.
- Divide the dough into equal – sized balls and smoothen the balls with your palms. This is best eaten fresh, since refrigeration makes these hard and dry.

XLII

Khaja

Khaja or Khajjaka, plain or sweet mentioned in *Manasollasa* (12th–century Sanskrit text composed by the Kalyani Chalukya king Someshvara III), was a wheat flour preparation fried in ghee. Khaja is believed to have originated from the eastern parts of the former state of Oudh and the former United Provinces of Agra and Oudh. This area presently corresponds to eastern districts of Uttar Pradesh and Western districts of Biharand is also native to state of Odisha as well as regions like Kutch and Andhra Pradesh. Refined wheat flour with sugar is made into layered dough, with or without dry fruit or other stuffing, and lightly fried in oil to make khaja.It is one of the very famous sweets of Odisha and is related to emotions of all Odia people. It is also offered as an offering in the Jagannath Temple, Puri.

Khajas from Silao and Rajgir in Bihar are almost entirely similar to Baklava, whereas the ones from Odisha and Andhra Pradesh are made with thicker pastry sheets, and are generally hard.The batter is prepared from wheat flour, mawa and oil. It is then deep fried until crisp. Then sugar syrup is made which is known as "*Paga*". The crisp croissants are then soaked in the sugar syrup until they absorb the sugar syrup. *Kaja of Kakinada*, a coastal town of Andhra Pradesh, is dry from outside and full of sugar syrup from inside and is juicy.

Khaja Mithai in Nepal are very popular in Maithali and Bhojpuri community. This sweet is most necessary item to celebrate weddings and *Chhat puja* in Nepal, Bihar and Uttar Pradesh.

Kakinada Kaja– sweetmeat in a shape of cylinder and color of brown — at first glance, looks dry and rather unappetizing. However, one bite and you will know what bliss is. When it is fresh, the outer casing is crispy and almost like a wafer. For first timers, the first bite surprises of the juicy, sugary syrup inside are a delightful treat. It is no wonder that it is eaten as a snack and served at weddings, and also forms a part of Thali meals, as it is a perfect complement to the spicy East Godavari cuisine. The credit for first making and selling it goes to *Chittipeddi Kotaiah*, who hails from Chinaparimi village, Tenali, Guntur District. In 1891 he came to Kakinada started a sweet shop named *Kotaiah Sweets* in the main market, it is still continued by the 5th generation of his descendants. There are a total of six branches, five at Kakinada and one at Rajahmundry.

Recipe:

Ingredients :

For dough–

- Maida – 1 cup
- Ghee– 2 tbsp
- Water– ¼ cup
- Oil– for deep frying

For sugar syrup–

- Sugar – 1½ cup
- Water – ¼ cup
- Gr.cardamom powder – ¼ tsp
- Lemon juice – 1 tsp

Method:

- Firstly, in a large bowl take 1 cup maida and add 2 tbsp ghee.
- Crumble and mix well making the flour is moist.
- Now add ¼ cup water and knead smooth and soft dough.
- Grease the dough with oil. Cover and rest for 15 minutes.
- Dust the dough with maida and roll with the rolling pin.
- Roll as thin as possible making sure to dust maida as required.
- Now cut the sides forming a large square/rectangle.
- Start to roll tightly from one side.
- Dust maida on each roll to prevent layers from sticking to each other.
- Roll the cylinder tight to remove any air gaps if present.
- Cut it into 1 inch pieces and slightly flatten.

- Fry on low–medium flame till they turn crispy and golden in colour.
- Immediately drop the fried khajas into the warm sugar syrup.
- Soak them in the syrup for 5 minutes.
- Finally, serve madatha khaja or store in an airtight container for 10–15 days.

XLIII
Khapse

Khapse or amjok is a deep–fried pastry type North Himachali biscuit that is traditionally prepared during the Tibetan/Sherpa New Year or Losar and weddings. With Tibetan Losar approaching, shops selling — ***khapse*** become more and more in the street of Lhasa City, and the festive atmosphere of Tibetan Losar is gradually thick. Tibetans call these beloved cookies mouth–eat, which gets straight to the point.

Cooks prepare massive quantities of khapse as offerings, as festive gifts, and to keep their mouths busy while preparing other holiday dishes in the kitchen. During Losar, khapse are often enjoyed with sweet tea or Tibetan butter tea. The dough for the khapse is usually made with flour, eggs, butter and sugar. Khapse is an indispensable food of Tibetan traditional festivals.

Tibetan dim sum: It is a kind of fried food which is made of white flour, yak butter, milk, sugar and other raw materials, with a variety of forms like ear, butterfly, bar, square and circle, etc., and is an essential in Tibetan family to greet Losar.

Recipe:

Ingredients:

- All–purpose flour – 4 cups
- Sunflower oil –½ cup
- Sugar /jaggery– 1/3 cup
- Full cream milk – 1 cup
- Sunflower oil – for deep frying

Method:

- Dissolve the sugar or jaggery in 1 cup of warm water.
- Combine flour, oil and sugar.
- Mix everything together to knead to smooth ball of dough.
- Roll out the dough to about a ¼ inch thickness. (When you roll it out you can put a little flour down on the rolling surface so that it won't stick, but not much. If you put too much extra flour, it will make the dough suck up too much oil while cooking.)
- Cut the dough in strips (maybe about an inch or a little less), then cut those strips into diagonal pieces.
- Slice a slot in the middle of each piece of dough.
- Pull one corner of the piece of dough through the slot in the middle, creating a twist.
- Fry them in small lots in sunflower oil till golden brown.

XLIV
Kheer

Kheer is a pudding, originating from the Indian subcontinent, made by boiling milk and sugar with one of the following– rice, broken wheat, tapioca, vermicelli, or sweet corn. It is flavoured with cardamom, raisins, saffron, cashews, pistachios, almonds or other dry fruits and nuts. It is typically served during a meal or as a dessert. The first mention of kheer, which historians say was derived from the Sanksrit word *kshirika* (meaning a dish prepared with milk), is found in the fourteenth century Padmavat of Gujrat, not as a rice pudding but a sweet preparation of jowar and milk. Back then using millets in pudding was quite common. Kheer is believed to have originated in the Lord Jagannath Temple, Puri, Orissa around 2,000 years ago where it was served as an offering to the gods. This practice spread throughout South Asia to various Hindi temples where the recipe was altered slightly based on the region. Today, there are distinct differences between the kheer produced in Eastern vs. Southern vs. Northern India. It also has many variations not as thick as kheer, called *meetha bhaat, payasam, payasa, or dudhpak.* The name *kheer* suggests that the dish came to India from the Middle East because sheer means milk in Farsi. Also, the fact that many Muslim communities in India make it with sewiyan (certainly a Middle Eastern import) suggests a West Asian or Arab origin.

Phirni–is also a type of kheer or rice pudding It is sometimes called as sheer, which stands for milk in Persian. It is enjoyed by people of many cultures and cuisines. This food traces its roots to the grain pottages of the Middle East. It is associated with good nutrition and easy digestion, and medical texts earlier owned its name, rather than cookery books. Itis a sweet milky dessert, supposed to be eaten cold, made with cornflour or rice flour, or sometimes both are used and usually flavoured with rose water and/or ground cardamom. The dish is embellished with chopped or ground almonds or cashew nuts. The history of Phirni takes us back a very long way; though there is no written evidence, still it's believed that Phirni seems to have originated in ancient Persia or the Middle East; and Mughals have introduced Phirni to India‖

Seviyan kheer– or vermicelli kheer is made from vermicelli, is very popular among the muslim culture and is prepared during Eid. This popular dish is famous among all the Indians from north to south. The *kheer* is made by dry roasting vermicelli to a golden brown color till a nice aroma starts to come from it and then milk and other flavorings are added to give a nice and creamy *kheer.*

Recipe of Rice Kheer:

Ingredients:

- Full cream milk – 5 cups
- Washed rice – ¼ cup
- Sugar – ½ cup
- Raisins – 10–12 nos.
- Green cardamoms – 4 nos.
- Blanched & shredded almonds – 10–12 nos.

Method:

- Boil the rice and milk in a deep pan.
- Simmer over low flame, stirring occasionally till the rice is cooked and the milk becomes thick.
- When done add sugar, raisins and cardamoms.
- Stir till sugar gets dissolved properly.
- Transfer into a serving dish and garnish with almonds.
- Serve hot or chilled.

XLV

Kheer Sagar

It is an Odia sweet dish that literally translates to ocean of milk in the Odia language. Also called *Angoori rasmalai*, this sweet has depiction in the Hindu mythological scripture about Lakshmi serving Vishnu and Madhusudana with it. Kheer sagara consists of marble–sized balls of chhena cheese soaked in sweetened, condensed milk. Saffron and cardamoms are the typical seasonings that are added to this dish. Khira sagara is typically served either at room temperature or slightly chilled. It is a Navratri especial sweet dish. This dish is probably Rasmalai's predecessor. However, the milk base in khira sagara is thicker, acquiring the consistency of rabri and no dry fruits added to it.

Recipe:

Ingredients:

For Chenna Balls

- Full cream milk – 3 cups
- Sooji/semolina– 1 tsp
- Powder sugar– 1 tbsp
- Gr. Cardamom powder – a pinch
- Juice of lemon– 1

For Ras (thickened milk)–

- Full cream milk –750 ml
- Sugar – ½ cup
- Mawa – ¼ th cup

- Gr. Cardamom powder – 4 no
- Saffron –few strands soaked in 2 tbsp of warm milk

Method:

- Boil 500 gms. milk in a heavy bottom pan. When milk boils reduce the heat add lemon juice and stir once.
- The milk will curdle and the whey will begin to separate.
- Strain the curdle milk through a muslin cloth lined above a colander.
- Wash the chenna under running water , tie the cloth and hang it for 20 minutes.
- But don't squeeze or press the knot to release extra water from the chenna.
- In the mean time boil rest of the milk in low flame, stir occasionally to prevent sticking to bottom.
- After 20 minutes take the chenna and start kneading it using the heels of your palm.
- Add sooji, powder sugar and cardamom powder.
- Keep kneading till your palm becomes oily.
- Make 15–17 equal sized tiny balls.
- Boil 2 cups of water in a big, wide pan.
- When water boils drop the balls on the boiling water.
- Let it boil for 5 minutes on high flame.
- Reduce the heat and boil for 15 minutes till the balls became double in size. Please note that there should be enough space so that balls can be double in size or you can make these in two batches.
- When milk reduced to half add mawa, cardamom powder, crushed saffron and sugar.
- Stir well. Be very careful so that milk doesn't stick to the bottom.
- Boil for 5 minute more.
- Chenna balls must be ready by now.
- Drop the chenna balls in reduced milk.
- Let it cook for 2–3 minutes.
- Switch off the flame, let it come to room temperature or chill in refrigerator before serving.

XLVI

Khubani ka Meetha

Khubani ka Meetha is a sinfully delicious dessert from Hyderabad, India. Usually served after a sumptuous meal, especially during festivals and weddings, Qubani ka Meetha is made of apricot, cooked in sugar and spices. It is a perfect blend of flavors sweet, sour and lusciously creamy. Qubani or Khubani is an Urdu word which means apricot and Meetha is anything sweet. It is believed that apricots were introduced to the Indian subcontinent by the Mughals through Persia and Afghanistan. Later on it was adopted by the Nizams of Hyderabad as their sweet delicacy. It is served in every occasions and festivals of elite class in Hyderabad and Telengana.

Recipe:

Ingredients:

- Dried apricots/khubani – 18–20
- Water1–1.5 cups
- Sugar (or per taste) – 1 tsp
- Milk – 1 cup
- Custard powder – 1½ tbsp
- Sugar – 1½ tbsp
- Sliced or chopped almonds – few

Method:

- Rinse the apricots well.
- Soak apricots in 1.5 cups water overnight—preserve this water because you will need it for cooking.

- Now, in a deep non–stick pan, combine chopped apricots and 1 cup of preserved water. Cook on a low to medium flame for about 15–20 minutes.
- Once you observe that the apricots have started becoming soft, mash them using a vegetable masher. If you feel that the mixture has become too dry, you can add more water.
- Now add 1 tsp sugar and mix well. Cook for another 4–5 minutes.
- Remove from flame and set aside.
- In a thick–bottomed pan, heat milk.
- As soon as the milk becomes warm, take about ¼ cup milk in a bowl. Add custard powder in it and mix well. Make sure there are no lumps in the mixture.
- When the milk comes to a boil, add sugar in it. Keep on stirring continuously.
- Once the sugar dissolves, add milk–custard mixture and cook on a medium flame for 8–10 minutes or till the custard thickens, while stirring continuously.
- Remove from flame and set aside.
- In a serving bowl/glass, put a portion of the prepared custard, top it with a portion of the khubani and finally top it with chopped almonds.
- Repeat the same procedure to make more servings.

XLVII

Koat Pitha

Mizoram's famous Koat Pitha is a delectable fritters recipe, which is easy–to–make and can be prepared at home without putting in much effort. Made with the goodness of rice flour, banana, powdered jaggery and oil. Koat Pithas are usually dry and can be packed for road trips, picnics and fairs. To increase the shelf life of this pitha recipe, you can store these pithas in a dry airtight container in a cool place. This non–messy pitha can be carried anywhere. The use of jaggery in this dish makes it a healthy choice and amps up the health quotient. This delectable recipe is served with a hot piping cup of tea.

Recipe:

Ingredients:

- Rice flour – 1 cup
- Ripe Bananas – 4 nos.
- Powdered jaggery– 1/3 cup
- Water – ¼ cup
- Salt – a pinch
- Sunflower Oil – for frying

Method:

- First dissolve the jaggery in water and pass it through a fine filter to remove the scum.
- Mash the bananas and keep them aside in a bowl.

- To the mashed banana, now add the jaggery water and rice flour and with a pinch of salt.
- Mix the Koat Pitha mixture until well combined and becomes a thick batter.
- Heat a pan with oil on medium heat and spoon a small amount of batter into the oil.Fry the Koat Pitha till it becomes golden and drain it on a paper towel.
- Serve as a delicious dessert after a light meal of *Sana Thongpa* and *Tan Ngan*, or as an evening tea time snack along with masala chai.

XLVIII

Kozhukatta

Kozhukatta or Kozhukkattai is a popular South Indian dumpling made from rice flour, with a filling of grated coconut, jaggery or chakkavaratti. Kozhukatta, although usually sweet, can sometimes be stuffed with a savory filling. Modak is a similar dish made in other parts of India. In Tamil Nadu, the dish is traditionally associated with the Hindu God Ganesha and is prepared as an offering (*naivedhya*) on the occasion of Vinayaka Chathurthi. In Kerala, it is popularly associated with Oshana Sunday celebrations of Saint Thomas Christians. The dish is prepared by mixing grated coconut with jaggery syrup, placing it inside dumplings of rice flour, and steaming the dumplings. Ghee, cardamom, finely ground roasted rice flour etc. may be added to enhance the taste and flavour of the filling. In Kerala, a variant of kozhukatta made with atta flour (instead of rice flour) and grated coconut is a staple breakfast among some groups.

Recipe:

Ingredients:

- Powdered rice – 1 cup
- Jaggery– 150 gms
- Coconut – 1 cup
- Water – as required
- Salt – pinch
- Gr. cardamom– 4 nos
- Clove – 1 piece
- Ghee – ½ tsp

Method:

- To prepare the dough– Boil one cup of water with salt. Add the boiled water to the rice flour and mix it with a wooden spatula/spoon. Knead until it forms smooth dough. Keep it aside for 5 minutes or till it is warm enough to handle. Knead the dough and make it into a soft ball. The consistency of the dough should be same as that of Idiyappam dough and also the dough should not be sticky.
- For the filling– Melt the jaggery with ¼ cup of water and strain it. Add the coconut to the filtered jaggery& mix well. Add ghee and cook till the liquid is dried up. Add crushed cardamom clove and remove from fire. Keep it aside.
- Make medium size balls out of the dough. Take one ball at a time and place it in your palm. Press it with the other hand and make it thin. Start folding it inwards in such a way that you get a cup shape. Place 1–2 tsp of the filling, cover it and roll it back into a ball. Repeat the process with the rest of the dough and filling.
- Steam the kozhukattas in appachembu/steamer for 9–10 minutes on medium flame. Keep it covered for 1 more minute. Serve warm.

XLIX
Kulfi

Kulfi a popular Indian frozen dairy dessert, has been called Indian ice cream and may have been invented by those ancient inhabitants of the Himalayas. The origin of kulfi dates back to the Mughal Empire that ruled India from the sixteenth to the eighteenth century. This ice cream was then prepared in the royal kitchens with ice that came from the mountains of the Himalayas. During the Mughal period, this mixture was flavoured with pistachios and saffron, packed into metal cones and immersed in slurry ice, resulting in the invention of Kulfi. Ain–e–Akbari, a detailed record of the Mughal emperor Akbar's administration, mentions use of saltpeter for refrigeration as well as transportation of Himalayan ice to warmer areas. One of the stories says that the original preparation of kulfi by the wife of Emperor Jahangir, Noorjahan is slightly different. She used to create and serve the frozen dessert by mixing sweetened milk with the pulp of many fruits to which was added imported crushed ice from the frozen Himalayan lakes. Later, it became popular as matka kulfi where vendors froze the dish in kulhars or earthen cups in salted ice.

Kulfi has similarities to ice cream in appearance and taste, but it is denser and creamier. It comes in various flavours. The more traditional ones are cream, rose, mango, cardamom, saffron , and pistachio. There are newer variations such as apple, orange, strawberry, peanut, and avocado. Unlike ice cream, kulfi is not whipped, resulting in a solid, dense frozen dessert similar to traditional custard–based ice cream.

Recipe:

Ingredients:

- Full cream milk – 1¼ lts
- Powdered Sugar – 1/3 cup
- Powdered gr. Cardamom – 4
- roughly chopped Pistachios – 8
- Saffron soaked in milk – few strands

Method:

- Heat milk in a wide bottomed pan and bring to a boil. Allow the milk simmer on medium flame till it reaches half its original quantity. Keep stirring in between.
- Add powdered sugar, cardamom powder and roughly chopped nuts. Mix well and keep simmering on medium flame, stirring till it further reduces to almost one–third of its original quantity. It will have a rabdi consistency and like very thick milk.
- Turn off flame and allow to cool.
- Once cool, place the mixture in the fridge for 2 hours. (This helps reduce the formation of ice crystals during freezing process).
- Place the empty kulfi molds in the freezer to chill.
- Next, remove the mixture from the fridge and whisk it well and place the mixture in the freezer. After an hour, take it out and whisk it well or keep mixing with a whisk/ladle to agitate it. Again place it back in the freezer.
- Remove it after 2 hours and again repeat the whisking process. At this stage, pour the whisked mixture into chilled kulfi molds and close the lids.
- Place the kulfi molds in the deep freezer and allow to set overnight or at least 8 hours.

L

Laddoo

Laddu or laddoo is a sphere–shaped sweet originated from the Sanskrit word Lattika. Laddus are made of flour, fat (ghee/butter/oil), and sugar, with other ingredients that vary by recipe, like chopped nuts or dried raisins. They are often served at festive or religious occasions. The history of laddu in India dates back to several centuries. *Sushruta*, also known as the "father of surgery" in India, is the author of *Sushruta Samhita* or The Compendium of Sushruta. The seminal work is often regarded as the basis of Ayurveda states that he created small edible balls made of ingredients like sesame seeds, jaggery and peanuts and inserted small dosages of medicine into them. This was done in order to make the drug easier to consume for the patient. Slowly and slowly Laddoo became an integral part and most preferred sweet in all kinds of celebration and occasions in India.

The long history of laddu in India explains the mind–boggling varieties as every region of India has its own take on laddus as dictated by the local availability of ingredients.

Boondi laddoo– laddoo made of small balls of besan called boondi, often served on festivals such as Raksha Bandhan and Diwali.

Motichoor laddu– is made from fine boondi where the balls are tiny and is cooked with ghee or oil.

Besan laddu– Besan laddu or Magaj is a popular Indian sweet dish made of besan (chickpea flour or gram flour), sugar and ghee. Besan is roasted in ghee till golden brown appearance with nutty fragrance. Then sugar is added to it. Pistachio pieces are also mixed in this mixture optionally. Sweet balls are then made from this mixture. It has a long shelf life.

Coconut laddu– laddoos made of grated coconut like *Naru* in West Bengal, Nariyal laddoo of North India.

Kobbari Kova Kajjikayalu– is also known as Kova Kobbari Laddu is a very old and classic Andhra sweet. The Telegu word for mawa is Kova. The outer layer of the sweet is made with khoya (milk solids) and sugar and the stuffing is so simple where we cook the fresh coconut and jaggery together to form a thick mixture.

Semolina or rava laddu– This a laddu prepared from rava (semolina), sugar and ghee. A variant on the recipe includes khoa cheese as an additional ingredient.

Till laddu– Till laddu made with sesame seeds and then mixed with cheese to form balls are famous in north India during the months of winter. Preferred in Northern India.

Gond ke laddoo– These laddus are called *Dinkache* ladoo in Marathi and gond ka laddu in Urdu. The main ingredient is gum arabic which is collected from the babul tree. Other ingredients include coconut, almonds, cashews, dates, spices such as nutmeg and cardamom, poppy seeds, ghee, and sugar.

Pori urundai – a crunchy, crisp, light, delicious laddoo made with puffed rice and jaggery.

Darbesh – Darbesh is a Bengali laddu. Darbesh is made with khoya or mawa , besan , sugar , ghee or oil and different nuts .

Recipe of Besan ke laddoo:

Ingredients:

- Ghee – ½ cup
- Coarse besan – 2 cup
- Sugar – 1 cup
- Gr. Cardamom – 4 pods
- Melon seeds – 2 tbsp
- Chopped cashew – 2 tbsp

Method:

- Firstly, in a large kadai heat ½ cup ghee and add 2 cup besan.
- Roast on low flame until the besan is well combined with ghee. Make sure to use coarse besan for grainy texture.
- Continue to roast on low flame. If the mixture turns dry, add a tbsp of more ghee.

- After 20 minutes, the besan starts to release ghee.
- Continue to roast until the besan turns golden brown and grainy. It may take approximately 30 minutes.
- Transfer the mixture to a large bowl, allowing cooling slightly.
- Meanwhile, dry roast 2 tbsp melon seeds and 2 tbsp cashew.
- Roast on low flame until the nuts turn crunchy.
- Add the roasted nuts to roasted besan ghee mixture.
- Take 1 cup sugar and 4 pods cardamom in a blender. You can alternatively use tagar or boora.
- Blend to a fine powder without adding any water.
- Once the besan is cooled (slightly warm) add in powdered sugar.
- Mix well making sure everything is well combined. Do not add sugar if the mixture is hot, as it will melt the sugar and makes mixture watery.
- Prepare a ball sized ladoo adjusting sugar as required.
- Finally, enjoy besan ladoo for 2 weeks in an airtight container.

LI

Lapsi

A sweet delicacy from the state of Gujarat, Maharashtra, Uttar Pradesh and Rajasthan. In Gujrat, it is also called *Kansar*. Unlike other regular Indian sweets, this is a healthy sweet dish and is made using broken wheat (Dalia), ghee and dried fruits along with some sugar. This dish is very simple, easy, delicious and fast to cook. Lapsi is nutritious as it is unrefined wheat and high in fiber and manganese. It is made and served in especial occasions like child naming ceremony, marriages, Navratri and Diwali.

Recipe:

Ingredients:

- Broken wheat– 2 cup
- Almonds– 3nos
- Water– 5 cups
- Powdered gr. Cardamom – 2 tbsp
- Raisins– 20nos
- Ghee – 1 ¼ cup
- Sugar – 1 ¼ cup
- Cashews – 10 nos

Method:

- Soak the raisins in water and keep aside till required further.
- Meanwhile blanch almonds, de–skin and chop.
- Roast broken wheat on medium flame till light brown in colour.

- Add water to the pan and let the broken wheat cook until it gets tender and the water has almost vaporized.
- Once the mixture has no water left in it, add sugar, cardamom powder, peeled and chopped almonds, soaked raisins, ghee, and water in the pan. Cook the mixture on low flame for about 10 minutes until the ghee is significantly visible at the sides of the pan.
- Once done remove the lapsi from flame and garnish it will the blanched almonds and cashews before serving.

LII
Lassi

Lassi is a popular traditional dahi (yogurt)–based drink that originated in the state of Punjab. Lassi is a blend of yoghurt, water, spices and sometimes fruit. Salted lassi is made by adding rock/table salt and spices, while sweet and mango lassis are like milkshakes. Traditionally, lassi is served in a handleless clay cup called a *kulhar*, and extra malai (clotted cream) may be spooned on top before serving. The drink is enjoyed chilled in various parts of India as great refreshment in hot weather. Lassi is not just a refreshing cold drink, it has several health benefits. In India, lassi is served during religious ceremonies too.

Lassi is served in various forms like–

Mango Lassi– It is one of the most popular variants of Indian lassi. Made with yogurt, mango pulp or fresh mango and water, this variety of lassi is delicious. It is served with nuts on top.

Sweet Lassi–Another variety of lassi is sweet lassi. It is the authentic form of this delicious drink. It is made by blending yogurt, water, spices and sugar. It is often flavored with rosewater, fruit juices and so forth.

Spicy Lassi–Made with yogurt, spices, fresh mint, salt and water, spicy lassi is one of my favorite choices. It is served with Indian dishes as it is known to improve digestion.

Mint Lassi–Different types of ingredients are used to prepare mint lassi. Mint leaves, cumin seeds, yogurt, water and salt are blended till the mixture becomes frothy. It is served chilled and garnished with chopped mint.

Chocolate Lassi– This is another delicious variety of lassi that is made with chocolate syrup, yogurt and water.

Apart from these varieties, lassi is prepared in different flavors to entice the taste buds.

Recipe:

Ingredients:

- Yogurt – 2 ½ cups
- Sugar – ½ cup
- Ice cubes – as required
- Milk optional – ½ cup
- Fresh cream as required

Method:

- Blend together yogurt and sugar for two minutes in a mixer/blender.
- Add ice cubes and blend for a minute more.
- If the mixture is too thick add a little milk and adjust consistency and blend once more.
- Pour into serving glasses from a height so as to form foam.
- Top with malai and serve chilled.

LIII

Madhurjan Thongba

Madhurjan Thongba is a traditional North Eastern dessert recipe for Manipur. The best thing about this sweet is the aromatic flavor of cardamom and bay leaf in it which provides this dish with a divine flavor.

Recipe:

Ingredients:

- Milk – 1 ½ cup
- Refined oil – 1 cup
- Bay leaf – 1 no
- Grated coconut – 2 tbsp
- Besan – 1 cup
- Sugar – 2 ½ tbsp
- Black cardamom – 1 tsp

Method:

- Prepare a thick besan batter by mixing together besan and little water.
- Deep fry small balls of the batter in oil till cooked and golden brown.
- Boil milk and add 2 tbsp. of sugar and bay leaf stirring constantly..
- Now gently add the fried besan balls in this milk mixture and cook for 3 to 4 minutes.
- Add the grated coconuts and cardamom powder and serve hot.

LIV
Makhan Mishri

Makhan Mishri, the most favorite all time liked of Lord Krishna. It is an essential item of the *Chappan bhog* (the traditional 56 items prepared to offer Bal Gopal) during the festival of Janamashtmi. A combination *makhan* (white butter) and *mishri* (rock sugar) is offered as Prasad. Consuming Makhan mishri everyday helps in mental growth and development. It is also known to enhance and sharpen memory. The daily intake of the Makhan Mishri mix in the morning helps to lubricate the joints and prevent stiffness.

Recipe:

Ingredients:

- Homemade white butter – 100 gm
- Mishri – 20 gm

Method:

- Put makhan in refrigerator to chill for half an hour.
- Grind mishri in a mixer to get coarsely powder.
- At the time of serving add coarsely grinded mishri to butter and mix well.
- Serve in individual bowls.

LV

Malpua

It's a dessert that is popular in nearly every street and household across Northern and Eastern India as a part of this legacy continues to be the oldest Indian mithai. The first reference of our very own malpua was made in the Rigveda, as "*Apupa*". Rigveda is the oldest of the four Vedas and talks about the recipe of Apupa that uses barley flour made in form of flat cakes, deep fried in ghee and then dipped in honey before serving. Parts of Bengal, Bihar, Orissa, Nepal and Bangladesh prepare the dessert for various festive occasions. Malpua is part of the Sakala Dhupa or morning food served to the lord Jagannath at the legendary Jagannath Temple in Puri, Orissa. Malpuas along with *Patishapta* are an intrinsic part of Poush or Makar Sankranti celebrations in Bengal. Malpuas are also prepared in Odia homes during *Raja sankranti.* Malpua is also an illustrious part of '*Chappan Bhog*' served to Lord Krishna on Janmashtami and Govardhan Puja.

Recipe:

Ingredients:

- All-purpose flour– 200 gm
- Fennel seeds– 1 tsp
- Powdered green cardamom– 1 tsp
- Ghee– 1 cup
- Water– 250 ml
- Khoya– 50 gm
- Semolina– 100 gm
- Baking powder – ½ tsp
- Milk –500 ml

- Sugar –250 gm
- Saffron –as required

Method:

- To prepare the sugar syrup, place water in a pan over medium flame. Add sugar in it and stir until fully dissolved.
- Then add 2–3 tsp milk and stir again, after a few minutes remove the scum that rises to the top. Once the sugar syrup is thick, remove the pan from the flame and keep aside.
- In a separate bowl mix maida, rava, khoya, baking powder, fennel seeds, cardamom powder and milk. Whisk it and ensure that the mixture has a pourable consistency and is not too thick. Once the batter is ready, keep it aside for few minutes so that the flavour of spices and herbs are fully absorbed.
- Now heat ghee in a pan over low flame. Pour a ladleful of the mixture and spread evenly. Keep the flame low and cook till it is light brown on both sides.
- Remove the cooked malpua and drain the excess ghee.
- Drop the malpua in sugar syrup and allow it to soak for 10 minutes. Repeat the same with the remaining batter. Drain the malpuas from the syrup, garnish with pistachios and serve hot.

LVI
Malai Paan

Malai pan or Balai ki Gilouri is a delicate sweet made with paper thin malai filled with mishri and dry fruits. During 1800s when tobacco and paan was prohibited during Nawaab Wajid Ali Shah's rule in Lucknow, this Balai ki Gilouri was made to replicate paan. Though it is a dessert, it was served just like paan decorated with silver varq. The beauty of r malai ki gilori is its melt – in – the – mouth quality and its delicate taste, especially the one with kesar ki mishri.

Recipe:

Ingredients:

- Milk – 200 ml
- Mawa – 1 tbs
- Pistachios – 3
- Cardamom Powder – a pinch
- Ghee – ½ tsp
- Sugar – 1 tsp
- Saffron – for garnish

Method:

- In a heavy bottomed pan, bring milk to boil.

- Reduce flame to low and allow the cream to form as a fine layer on top. Do not stir milk.
- Once the cream is thick enough, remove it gently with a spatula or slotted spoon. It is quite tricky.
- Instead you can refrigerate the milk at this stage so that the cream thickens and easy to remove.
- Roast mawa, sugar and pistachios in ghee for a few minutes.
- Take the cream, spread it out on a plate, place some filling inside and fold it as you fold a paan.
- Garnish with saffron, silver varq and pistachios and serve immediately or serve it chilled.

LVII

Mambazha Pradhaman

Mambazha pradhaman is one of a delicious recipe made with ripe mangoes. This recipe is typically served as a sweet dish during Onam season. As in the case of other pradhaman recipes jaggery and coconut milk is used for a delicious flavour. This recipe has a brownish orange colour. The use of fried coconut bits, raisins and cashew nuts increases the taste.This nutritious dessert is prepared with ripe mangoes, jaggery, ginger powder, cardamom powder, milk and healthy nuts like cashewnuts and raisins.

Recipe:

Ingredients:

- Sweet Ripe Mangoes – 3 big
- Mango pulp – 2 cups
- Powdered Jaggery – 3 or 4 big cubes
- Dried ginger powder – ¼ tsp
- Cardamom powder– 3/4 to 1 tsp
- Thin Coconut milk – around 2 cups
- Thick Coconut Milk – ½ cup
- Cashews – 15
- Raisins – a handful
- Ghee – 3 to 4 tbsp
- Water – 1 cup

Method :

- Peel the mangoes and dice it into small pieces.

- Boil the jaggery in 1 cup of water to make thick syrup.
- Heat 2 tbsp ghee in a heavy bottomed pan and saute the mango pieces until it changes color.
- Mash the mango pieces as it gets cooked. Keep on stirring so that it doesn‘t stick to the pan.
- Slowly add the mango pulp to the pan and continue sautéing for 5 – 7 minutes.
- Add the jaggery syrup to the pan and keep on stirring until it thickens. This will take some time until it reaches a thick consistency (*Varattiya Paruvam*). So please be patient at this stage.
- Reduce heat and add thin coconut milk to the pan, stirring continuously.
- Now add the dried ginger powder and cardamom powder and mix well.
- Simmer for 5 – 7 minutes and then add thick coconut milk. Simmer for a few more minutes and remove from stove top. Do not allow it to boil.
- Heat 1 tbsp ghee in a pan and fry the raisins and cashews for a few minutes. Pour it over the pradhaman.

LVIII

Mawa Bati

Mawa Bati is a rich mithai originated in Madhya Pradesh. It is made by stuffing a mava based dough with a rich mixture of nuts and mava, and deep-frying the delicate, stuffed balls till golden brown. These Mava Batis are then soaked in sugar syrup for a while and served warm. It is similar to Mawa kachoris of Rajasthan, but are little smaller. The idea of preparing of these bati came from sweet samosas which are famous in West Bengal. Initially mawaa batis incorporated all the broken pieces of other methais which could not be sold. These pieces were mixed together and enveloped with maida dough, deep fried and soaked in sugar syrup, but now they are made with different stuffings.

Recipe:

Ingredients:

- Khoya – 200 gm
- Maida – 400 gm
- Oil – 350 ml
- Sugar – 200 gm
- Water – 300 ml
- Cashew – 6 nos
- Almond – 6 nos
- Cardamom powder – ½ tsp
- Salt – Pinch

Method:

- Prepare one string sugar syrup.
- Knead dough with maida, pinch of salt and 100 ml water in a medium sized bowl.
- Divide the dough into small–sized balls.
- Mix together khoya, cashew, almond, cardmon powder, Take the already prepared khoa and mix chopped dry fruits into it.
- Take 1 ball, make a small hole with index finger then keep on spreading until it gains a bowl shape. Then fill the khoya and close it by twisting and pressing it between your palms.
- Heat the oil in a kadhai and side by prepare 1 string sugar syrup. Gently lower the mawa bati in hot oil. Cook it until it becomes golden brown in low to medium flame.
- After frying them put into sugar syrup and immediately transfer them in plate.
- Tempting Mawa bati is ready to be served.

LIX
Mihindana

Mihindana is an Indian sweet from Burdwan, West Bengal, India. Mihidana, described as the micro cousin of the traditional Boondi, is derived from two words, Mihi meaning fine, and Dana, meaning grain.

According to Late Nagendranath Nag, his grand–father Late Khettranath Nag first invented special Mihidana in Bardhaman during the regime of Maharaja Late Mahatabchand Bahadur. Seventy two years after this invention the name Mihidana earned its reputation all over India after the arrival of Lord Curzon in Bardhaman and his appraisal this sweet. On invitation of Maharaja Vijaychand Mahatab Lord Curzon visited Bardhaman on 19 August, 1904. To memorize the welcome lunch of Lord Curzon, Maharaja ordered Vairabchandra Nag, a sweet–maker of the town, to prepare something new and unique which would amaze the Lord. Vairabchandra Nag undertook the responsibility and introduced Mihidana. Lord Curzon was surprised to have such unique sweet and praised and thanked Vairabchandra Nag in the certificate given to him saying he never had such sweet ever before. Thereafter, the quality and name of this sweet reached all over the country and abroad. Late Nagendranath Nag, son of Late Vairabchandra Nag, broadcast this incident in Radio on 15 November, 1976. The bright yellow, petite, round–shaped sweet is known the world over and loved by gourmet. On March 31, 2017, Mihidana were both accorded the official GI tags.

Recipe:

Ingredients:

- Besan – 1 cup

- Water – 3/4th cup –1 cup
- Baking powder – Pinch
- Food color – pinch
- Salt – pinch

For Sugar Syrup:

- Sugar – 1 cup
- Water – 1 cup
- Green cardamom – 2
- Cinnamon – a small stick
- Ghee – 1 tea spoon

Method:

- Make medium thick sugar syrup with the ingredients mentioned.
- Make batter with the ingredients mentioned for batter. The batter should be medium thick. It must not be thin or else you won't have the perfect shape.
- Heat oil in a kadai. Hold the strainer just 2 inches above the hot oil.
- Now pour a little amount of batter onto the strainer with a spoon and from the back of the spoon press a little. It should fall with intervals, so little amount of batter one at a time .
- Fry the mihidaanas or small bundis until little crispy.
- Remove them from the oil with another spoon.
- When all the batter is exhausted, all the mihidaanas are fried, take little amount from it to crush into powder. Not too much a little amount.
- Put the remaining mihidaanas in the hot sugar syrup until they get soft. Remember the syrup should be boiling hot.
- Cook the boondis at very low flame for at least 5/6 minutes until the boondis absorbed almost all the syrup and turned very soft.
- Now while they are hot transfer half of them into the food processor and blend.
- Now transfer it to a bowl. Mix with the crushed boondis/ mihidaanas.
- Grease your hand with oil/ghee and make spherical laddus.

LX

Mishti Doi

The humble Mishti Doi may not involve the precision and craft that goes into making most popular across West Bengal, Orissa, Bihar and Bangladesh. Mishti Doi is a fermented sweet curd made by thickening milk and is sweetened with jaggery. It differs from the plain yogurt because of the technique of preparation. This mixture is placed in a traditional clay or earthen pot, to keep it cool. The moisture contained by its porous walls not only further thickens the yoghurt, but simultaneously also produces the right temperature for the growth of the culture. Mishti Doi is not only served as dessert but traditionally made for religious and festive occasions including weddings. This dish is usually sweetened with sugar. Sometimes caramelized sugar or date jaggery (*nolen gur*) is the choice of sweetener and this gives the yogurt a golden or reddish colour where this yogurt is then also referred to as Laal Mishti Doi where '*laal*' means red.

Recipe:

Ingredients:

- Full cream milk – 1ltr
- Sugar – 8 tbsp
- Yogurt (curd) – 1 tbsp
- Earthen pot (optional)– 1

Method:

- Pour the milk in a thick bottom vessel and start heating over low flame

- As it starts boiling add 4 tbsps of sugar and keep on simmering till the volume is reduced to little less than half
- Take the remaining sugar with 2 tbsps of water and heat till the sugar melts and attains a golden brown color
- Gradually add the molten sugar over the milk and boil for another 15 minutes over low flame
- Take out of flame and let it become lukewarm
- Pour the milk over the earthen pot and add the yogurt
- Keep the pot in a cool dry place, and let the yogurt set over night
- Refrigerate the set dahi and serve as a dessert

LXI
Modak

A Modak or Modakalu is a sweet dumpling popular in India and is usually made during the auspicious festival of Ganesh Chaturthi. Modak is an Indian sweet popular in many parts of India. The sweet filling on the inside of a modak consists of freshly grated coconut and jaggery while the outer soft shell is made from rice flour or wheat flour mixed with maida flour. Modak can be fried or steamed. The steamed version (called *ukdiche modak)* is often eaten hot with ghee. It is called modak in Marathi, Konkani and in Gujarati languages, *modhaka* in Kannada, *modhakam* or kozhakkattai in Tamil and *kudumu* in Telugu. Today fusion recipes are available and one can add chocolate, coconut, semolina and even dry–fruits.

Recipe:

Ingredients:

- Coconut, grated – 1 cup
- Jaggery– 1 cup
- Nutmeg – a pinch
- Saffron – a pinch

For the shell:

- Water – 1 cup
- Ghee – 1tsp
- Rice flour – 1 cup

Method:

Prepare filling:

- Heat a pan; add the grated coconut and jaggery.
- Stir for about five minutes. Add the nutmeg and saffron, mix well.
- Cook for another five minutes and keep aside.

Prepare modak–

- In a deep dish, boil water with ghee. Add the salt and flour. Mix well.
- Cover the dish and cook till its half done.
- Spread some ghee on the base of a steel bowl and while the dough is still hot, knead it well.
- Now take a little dough, roll it into a ball, flatten it well, and shape the edges into a flower pattern.
- Put a spoonful of the filling onto the dough and seal it.
- Put the dumplings in a muslin cloth and steam them for 10– 15 minutes. Serve.

LXII

Mohan Thaal

Mohan thal is a traditional mithai of Gujarat and Rajasthanand is often prepared during Janmashtmi, Navaratra and Diwali. It is believed that this dish was very much liked by Lord Krishna aka *Mohan*; hence it was named Mohan thal. It is a traditional mithai with the rich flavour and melt–in–the–mouth texture of ghee–roasted besan. This sweet is prepared through a technique called *dhrabo*, which is crumbing the besanand mixing it with milk and ghee,and laminating it. Then it is slowly passed through a strainer so it forms micro clusters that give Mohanthal its signature texture – crunchy bits of the 'crumble' embedded in a soft fudgy base. After the crumble is made, it is cooked in ghee till it reaches the golden brown in color.

Recipe:

Ingredients:

- Gram flour – 500 gms.
- Ghee – 300 gms.
- Milk –½ cup
- Grated mava – 250 gms.
- Sugar – 350 gms.
- Powdered gr. cardamom – 1tbsp
- Saffron – ½ tsp.
- Finely sliced almonds and pistachio nuts – 25 gms.

Method:

- Mix together 50 gms. of ghee and flour with a fork nicely.
- Add in the milk, mix thoroughly using a fork.
- Sieve this mixture through a large holed sieve. The larger grains which are sieved through help to give the mohanthal a lovely grainy texture.
- Heat the remaining ghee and stir in the flour. Keep stirring and cooking the mixture until the flour looks golden brown.Add khoya, cardamons and nuts and cook till the mixture turns smooth.
- Make 2 string consistency sugar syrup using 2 cups of water.
- Add syrup to the cooked flour and mava and keep on stirring till the mixture turns thick.
- Add a couple of drops of saffron essence. Keep stirring for a couple of minutes.
- Pour the mixture in a greased dish similar to a flan dish (thali) and level the surface using a flat spoon. Sprinkle more sliced nuts to decorate the mohanthal.
- Let the Mohanthal cool down. This could take several hours so cover the thali and leave it in a cool place. Then cut the Mohanthal into small rectangle or diamond shapes and store in air–tight container.

LXIII

Mysore Pak

Mysore pak is an Indian sweet prepared in ghee that is popular in Southern India and is traditionally served in baby showers, weddings and other festivals of southern India. It originated in the Indian state of Karnataka. It is made of generous amounts of ghee, sugar, gram flour, and often cardamom. The texture of this sweet is similar to a buttery and dense cookie. Mysore pak was first prepared in the kitchens of the Mysore Palace during the regime of Krishna Raja Wadiyar IV, by a palace cook named *Kakasura Madappa*. Madappa made a concoction of gram flour, ghee and sugar. When asked its name, Madappa had nothing in mind, simply called it the *'Mysuru pak'*. Pak (or paka, more precisely) in Kannada means sweet.

Recipe:

Ingredients:

- Sugar – 2 cup
- Baking soda – 1 pinch
- Besan – 1 cup
- Ghee – 3 cup
- Water – 1 cup

Method:

- Add 1 cup of ghee in a pan and heat it over medium flame. Once the ghee is sufficiently hot, add gram flour in it and fry it for few minutes properly.
- In another pan, boil the sugar with water till it reaches a one string consistency.

- When the sugar syrup is prepared, add the fried gram flour in it and stir well till it thickens.
- Heat the remaining ghee and gently add the gram flour mixture. Keep stirring all the time so that no lumps are formed.
- When the ghee starts to rise up from the sides and begins to separate, add the baking soda.
- Stir and pour into a greased plate. Gently spread the mixture and allow it to cool. Before it hardens fully, slice into desired shapes.
- Store in an airtight container, and serve when you like.

LXIV
Naankhatai

Nankhatai are shortbread biscuits, originating from the Indian subcontinent, popular in Northern India and Pakistan. The word Nankhatai is derived from Persian word *Naan* meaning bread and "*Khatai*" from an Dari Persian word meaning Biscuit. In Afghanistan and Northeast Iran, these biscuits are called *Kulcha–e–Khataye*. Kulcha is a type of Indian bread similar to Naan.

Nankhatai is believed to have originated in Surat in the 16th century, the time when Dutch and Indians were the important spice traders. A Dutch couple set up a bakery in Surat to meet the needs of local Dutch residents. When the Dutch left India, they handed over the bakery to an Iranian. The bakery biscuits were disliked by the locals. To save his business he started selling dried bread at low prices, Mr. Dotivala, quite the entrepreneur and experimenter, then created the *Farmasu Surti Batasa* or butter biscuits, which are still very popular. He also created the now famous Nankhatai as an interpretation of a local sweet from Surat called 'Dal' and also probably inspired by the Irani or Afghan Khatai. Nankhatai was also called as "*Nuncatie*" by the British.

Recipe:

Ingredients:

- Maida – 1 cup + 2 tbsp
- Semolina – 2 tbsp
- Baking Soda – ¼ tsp
- Sal – a pinch
- Unsalted Butter (or ghee) – ½ cup

- Powdered Sugar – ½ cup
- Gr. Cardamom Powder – ¼ tsp
- Finely chopped Pistachio – 1 tbsp

Method:

- To powder the sugar, grind it in a small jar of a mixer grinder or a blender. Sieve (1 cup + 2 tbsps) maida in a bowl, add 2 tbsps semolina, ¼ tsp baking soda and a pinch of salt. Mix them with a spoon.
- Take ½ cup butter or ghee and powdered sugar in another bowl.
- Beat them using a wire whisk or hand mixer until smooth and soft. Add ¼ tsp cardamom powder and beat again.
- Add sieved dry ingredients.
- Mix well and make a dough using hand. If the dough looks very greasy, add 1–2 tbsps more flour and mix well (don't add too much flour).
- Preheat oven to 350 degree Fahrenheit (180 degree Centigrade) for at least 10 minutes. Divide dough into 18 equal portions and make round shaped balls from it. Line a parchment pepper or an aluminum foil over baking tray. Take each ball and press a little between your palms to give it a patty like shape and place it over baking tray.
- Top each one with a little bit of finely chopped pistachio and press gently with your finger. Keep enough space between each cookie because it will expand in size during baking.
- Place baking tray in preheated oven and bake at 350 degree Fahrenheit (180 degree Centigrade) for around 15–18 minutes or until cookie starts to turn light golden in color.
- Remove baking tray from oven and transfer cookies over cooling rack (or wire rack). Cookies will be soft at this time but they will turn crispy and hard (not rock hard) as they cool down. Once at room temperature, they are ready to enjoy.

LXV

Nap Naang

Nap Naang is an exotic pudding recipe from the North Eastern state of Nagaland which tastes absolutely lip–smacking. This exotic dish is essentially a black rice pudding cooked using only 4 ingredients, black rice, milk, sugar and water. This delicious pudding has a rich texture and a nutty flavour that will be relished by people of all ages. Moreover, there is zero oil or butter used in the preparation of this delicacy which makes it fit for consumption even if you are on a weight watchers diet.

Recipe:

Ingredients:

- Black sticky rice – ¾ cup
- Water – 1 cup
- Milk – 2 ½ cups
- Sugar – ½ cup

Method:

- Wash the rice and soak it for 4–6 hrs or overnight in water.
- In the pressure cooker, add the rice (drained) with about 1 cup of water and 2 cups of milk.
- Cook until the cooker lets out 4–5 whistles (about 15–20 minutes). Then let the pressure release.
- Transfer the rice to the pan and add the sugar.
- Let it come to a boil and then simmer for about 5 minutes.
- Add the remaining ½ cup of milk and mix.

- Simmer until it reaches the required consistency and then let the pudding cool.
- Serve black rice pudding cold or at room temperature.

LXVI

Narkol Naru

Narkol Naru or Narikel Naru is a ball – shaped sweet from Bengal. It is made from Jaggary (gur) or sugar and coconut and is served during Durga puja, Lakshmi Puja, Poush Parbon (Makar Sankranti), and several other occasions. Narkol Naru in real life is not filled with anything. They are kind of sticky and sweet and brown (when made with gur) and off white (when made with sugar). The smell of cardamom, gur and coconut is divine and some might say that it is exotic.

Recipe:

Ingredients:

For 'chini' (sugar) 'naru':

- Freshly grated coconut – 200 gms
- Sugar – 200 gms
- Khoya (optional) – ½ cup
- Ghee – 1 tbsp
- Cardamom powder (optional) – ½ teaspoon

For 'gur' (jaggery) 'naru':

- Freshly grated coconut – 200 gms
- Jaggery – 150 gms
- Ghee – 1tbsp

For chini (sugar) naru:

- In a wok or kadhai, heat 1 tablespoon ghee.
- As the ghee smokes, add the grated coconut and stir for 2 minutes.
- Add the sugar along with khoya and mix well.
- Stir frequently until the sugar melts completely and has mixed with the grated coconut. Be careful about letting the sugar – coconut mix burn.
- Once the coconut mixture is sticky and can be shaped into balls, remove from the flame and set aside until it is warm. (To check whether the coconut mixture is cooked enough, scoop a tiny portion into your palm and shape it into a ball. If the shape holds, your coconut mixture is ready.)
- Let the mixture warm for a minute or two before forming small balls with it. A cool mixture will not allow you to shape so be careful.
- Serve fresh or store in airtight containers for 8 – 10 days.

For gurer (jaggery) naru:

- In a wok or kadhai, heat 1 tablespoon ghee.
- As the ghee smokes, add the grated coconut and stir for 2 minutes.
- Add the jaggery and mix well.
- Stir frequently until the jaggery melts completely and the coconut has taken a brown hue. Be careful about letting the jaggery – coconut mix burn.
- Once the coconut mixture is sticky and can be shaped into balls, remove from the flame and set aside until warm. (To check whether the coconut mixture is cooked enough, scoop a tiny portion into your palm and shape it into a ball. If the shape holds, your coconut mixture is ready.)
- Let the mixture warm for a minute or two before forming small balls with it. A cool mixture will not allow you to shape so be careful.
- Serve fresh or store in airtight containers for 8 – 10 days.

Note – If at any point you feel the naru mixture is not sticky enough, add some crumbled khoya and mix it well.

LXVII

Obbattu

Also called *Puran poli* is a sweet paratha. The various names for the flatbread include Puran poli or *Vedmi* in Gujarati, Puran poli in Marathi, *Uppittu* in Malayalam and Tamil, *Baksham* or *Bobbattu* or *Oliga* in Telugu and *Polae* for much thinner version in Telangana, *Holige* or *Obbattu* in Kannada, *Ubbatti* or simply *Poli* in Konkani. This sweet is prepared during auspicious occasions and during important festivals like Ugadi, Holi, Padwa, Diwali, Holi, Ganesh Chaturthi and others. It just looks like any other roti but is stuffed with a delicious sweet fillings made of channa dal and jaggery. The stuffing is made in many variations region wise in different traditional ways. In south coconut and jaggery, chopped cashew nuts are stuffed.

Recipe:

Ingredients:

- Flour–1 cup
- Sugar–1½ cup
- Powdered green cardamom – 3 nos.
- Salt–1 pinch
- Milk–4 tbsp
- Rice flour–2 tsp
- Chana dal–1 ½ cup
- Ghee– ½ cup
- Water – ¼ cup
- Refined oil –as required
- Nutmeg powder– ½tsp

Method:

- Take a glass bowl and mix flour with water in it. Knead well to make a stiff dough. Cover the dough and keep aside for 1 hour.
- Now take a pressure cooker and add chana dal and water in it. Put the cooker on the gas and heat it over high flame. Pressure cook the dal and once it's done, strain the excess water.
- Transfer the dal in a bowl and allow it to cool. Once the dal has cooled, add it in a pan and heat it over moderate flame. Add sugar along with ½ tbsp of ghee. Keep stirring. Cook on low flame till the gram mixture is soft and sticky. Once it's done, turn off the flame and keep the mixture aside.
- Now knead the dough again, adding salt, water and oil, little at a time, till the dough becomes pliable. Grind the dal and sugar mixture to a smooth consistency adding a little milk if it is too dry. Add cardamom powder and nutmeg powder.
- Now take a lime–sized lump of the dough and a little larger lump of the dal mixture. Roll out two rounds from the dough on a board sprinkled with rice flour, into flat rounds of about 7 inch in diameter.
- Cover the rolled dough round with the dal mixture, leaving half an inch at the edges, and then cover this with the second round. Roll again over this to seal them together, pinching the edges to seal well. Roll out like a thick chapati.
- Heat ghee on a hot griddle and put the puran poli on it. Keep pressing and turning it so that it cooks well on both sides. Keep adding ghee all around to brown it evenly without sticking to the griddle. Serve hot and pair with kheer, sewiyan, tea or coffee.

Palathalikalu is a traditional sweet dish from Guntur region of Andhra Pradesh made of handmade rice noodles, milk, jaggery and ghee. It is a special dish offered as Naivedyam or prasadam not only during Shankranti, Ganesh chathurthi and Polala amavasya but also during other Andhra festivals. —*Pala*‖ meaning made with milk and *Thalikalu* meaning noodles are prepared with rice flour in the shape of long cylinders. These are then cooked in thickened milk, sweetened with Jaggery, flavored with cardamom and finally garnished with fried nuts.

Recipe:

Ingredients:

- Milk – 1 litre
- Jaggery– 250 gm
- Cardamom powder – 1 tsp
- Sago – 50 gms
- Rice – 250 gms
- Cashews – 50 gms
- Ghee – 6 tsp
- Salt – a pinch

Method:

- Soak rice in water overnight and grind to a flour the next day.
- Heat ghee in a pan; fry cashew nuts and set aside.
- Mix rice flour, a little jaggery, salt, hot milk in a bowl to a dough and set aside.

- Boil milk with a cup of water in a vessel and add sago and cook so that sago becomes translucent.
- Place the dough in a (chickli press) and press the contents in to the milk.
- Cook on a low flame for a few minutes and now finish off with adding jaggery, ghee, cardamom powder and allow it to simmer for 5 minutes.
- Allow the palathalikalu to rest for few minutes and enjoy.

LXIX
Panasa Thonalu

Also called *Sampangi Poovulu* or *Flower Kaja* is a traditional Andhra sweet recipe and it got the name because of its flower shape. Panasa thonalu literally means Jackfruit bulbs in Telugu and it is also called as Sampangi Poolu or Flower Kaja. Its an especiality of Dussera festival.

Recipe:

Ingredients:

- Maida – ¼ kg
- Butter – 2 tbsp
- Jaggery – 200 gm
- Gr. cardamom powder – 2 tsp
- Oil – for deep Fry
- Ghee – 1 tbsp
- Salt – ½ tbsp
- Water – for making a dough

Method:

- Prepare sugar syrup by adding water to sugar and boil it until it reaches half string consistency.Switch off the flame and keep the syrup warm. Add cardamom powder to it and mix well.
- In a bowl add maida, salt and ghee and mix until it resembles the bread crumbs.
- Sprinkle water and knead it into smooth dough and cover it and leave it aside for half an hour.

- Knead the dough again and make small gooseberry sized balls out of maida dough.
- Roll each ball into a thin poori size of 3– 3.5" diameter.
- Use a sharp knife and make slits lengthwise leaving both the sides intact as shown in the picture.
- Now gently roll it like a mat and twist the edges to form poolu and arrange them in a plate. You can even do them like saree pleats and form like a chocolate.
- Meanwhile heat oil and drop a small ball of dough, if it rises to the top means it indicates the oil is hot enough to deep fry.
- Keep the flame on low–medium and deep fry 3–4 thonalu at a time until they turn golden brown. Remove them using a slotted spoon and drain them on a tissue paper or in the colander.
- Put it in the warm sugar syrup and soak it for 4–5 mins or until the next batch is fried.
- Remove them with a slotted spoon and arrange on a flat plate to let them dry slightly.
- Repeat the process to fry all the thonalu.
- Once they are slightly dried you can store them in an air tight container.

LXX
Parippu Payasam

This parippu pradhaman is a popular payasam in Kerala made with moong dal, jaggery and coconut milk as main ingredients. This gives nice volume and easy to cook too so best when serving for a crowd. It is a Perfect sweet dish to celebrate any special occasion like Onam. The prasadam is served to lord Vishnu in an honour that he killed the famous and notorious Mahabali the Asura.

Recipe:

Ingredients:

- Split yellow moong dal – ½ cup
- Water – 2 cups
- Jaggery– 1 cup
- Thin coconut milk – 1/3 cup
- Thick coconut milk – ½ cup
- Dry ginger powder – 1/8 tsp
- Jeera powder – 1/8 tsp
- Cardamom powder – a pinch
- Cashews (broken) – 5 nos
- Coconut pieces – 1.5 tbsp
- Melted ghee – 1 tbsp

Method:

- In a pressure cooker heat a tbsp of ghee – first add cashews fry till golden brown, set aside.

- Then add coconut pieces and fry till golden brown, set aside.
- Now add moong dal and roast for few mins until fragrant, do not let it brown.
- Add water and pressure cook for 2 whistles in low medium flame. Switch off.
- Let the pressure release by itself, now open and mash it up well with a ladle.Now place it in flame and add jaggery syrup, mix well.
- Extract coconut milk. First add thin coconut milk and let it boil and cook for 5mins in low flame.
- Cook until the payasam is slightly thick. Now add thick coconut milk. Mix well.
- Add jeera powder, dry ginger powder and cardamom powder, roasted cashews and coconut pieces, mix it and switch off.
- Serve hot

LXXI

Pateesa (Son Papri)

Pateesa also known as son papri, sohan papdi or shonpapdi is a popular Indian dessert. It has a crispy, threadlike texture that breaks in flakes but it can also be served in the form of layered squares. It was traditionally sold loose in a rolled paper cone, but modern industrial production has led it to be sold in tightly formed cubes. With the popularity of the sweet, newer flavors such as mango, strawberry, pineapple and chocolate have been introduced.

Soan papdi is said to have originated in India, specifically from west Maharashtra; spread across Gujarat, Punjab, Uttar Pradesh, and Rajasthan also having been proposed as potential origins. The origin of the sweet is unknown so it is associated with several different cultures. It can be eaten hot, cold, or even at room temperature. The main ingredients of this sweet include gram flour (also known as besan), all- purpose flour, ghee, milk and cardamom as a flavoring.

Recipe:

Ingredients:

- Gramflour – 1¼ cup
- Plain flour (maida) – 1¼ cup
- Ghee – 250 gms.
- Sugar – 2 ½ cups
- Water – 1 ½ cup
- Milk – 2 tbsp.
- Crushed cardamom seeds – ½ tsp.
- Charmagaz – 2 tsp.

- Thin polythene sheet – 4 squares cut

Method:

- Sift both flours together. Heat ghee in a heavy saucepan. Add flour mixture and roast on low till light golden. Keep aside to cool a little, stirring occasionally. Prepare syrup simultaneously.
- Make syrup out of sugar, water and milk to 2 ½ thread consistency.
- Pour at once into the flour mixture.
- Beat well with a large fork till the mixture forms threadlike flakes.
- Pour onto a greased surface or thali and roll to 1 thickness lightly.
- Sprinkle the charmagaz seeds and crushed cardamom and gently press down with palm.
- Cool, cut into 1 squares, wrap individually into square pieces of thin plastic sheet.

LXXII
Patishapta

A traditional pancake like recipe, Patishapta is a popular Bengali dessert. The festival of rice harvest in Bengal, 'poush sankranti' is celebrated by relishing this most delicious sweet. The final dish is a rolled pancake made of maida that is stuffed with a filling often made of coconut, milk, cream, and jaggery from the date palm. Waiting for Poush Sankranti for their fill of delicious patishapta is something all children in Bengali households would relate too. Not just Sankranti, one can spot the delicacy on festive occasions such as *Pohela Boishakh* (Bengali New Year) too. P*atishapta* can be called as the Indian cousin of French thin and crispy crepes. Stuffed with delectable jaggery, and grated coconut filling, *Patishapta* is one of the forms of *Pitha* which is famous across East India territory.

Recipe:

Ingredients:

For the batter:

- Maida – 1 cup
- Sooji – 1 cup
- Milk – 1 cup
- Sugar – 2 or 3 tsp
- Salt – ½ tsp (optional)
- Oil to cook the patishapta

For the filling:

- Grated fresh coconut– 2 cup

- Sugar – 1 cup
- Cashew nuts – 1 tbsp
- Raisins – 1 tbsp
- Cardamom – 7 to 8

Method:

For the filling:

- Heat a pan, then add grated coconut, sugar and stir , saute the coconut on a low flame for 3 to 4 minutes.
- After sugar melted and coconut became soft than add Cashew, Raisins, cardamon powder and mix well.
- Once this mixture becomes brown then our coconut mixture is ready for Patishapta filling.

For the patishapta:

- Take refined flour in any big bowl. Add semolina, sugar, salt and milk into it and make a smooth batter. But mix it carefully not making any lumps.
- Keep the batter aside for 10 minutes.
- Take a non – stick flat pan or tava. Put a little oil.
- Now take 2 to 3 tbsp batter and spread it over the tawa and spread the mix on the pan till it makes a circular shape.
- Now put the filling as per your pathshapta size or taste wise at the center of it and roll it.
- Then press it gently with the spatula to give it a shape of a Frankie or roll.
- Now your patishapta is ready to serve.
- Serve warm or cold any ways this patishapta will be tasty.

LXXIII

Peda

Peda or Pera is a sweet dish hailing from the Indian subcontinent. It is an essential part to celebrate any joyous occasion in India. Be its Diwali, Rakhi, Ganpati, somebody got promoted, baby's arrival and the list goes on. Being considered as an auspicious sweet, Peda are also served as prasad or prasadam in religious services.It originated from Mathura, Uttar Pradesh, India. Usually prepared in thick, semi–soft pieces, its main ingredients are khoa, sugar and traditional flavorings including cardamom seeds, pistachio nuts and saffron. Its colour varies from a creamy white to a caramel colour. The word peda is also generically used to mean a sphere of any doughy substance such as flour or khoa. Thakur Ram Ratan Singh of Lucknow who migrated to Dharwad (in the present–day Karnataka) in the 1850s introduced pedas there. This distinct variety is now famous as the Dharwad pedha. Kandi Peda from Satara in Maharashtra is another variety of peda. Simultaneously, another origin, practice of Peda making, some unique varieties, and spread of this tradition may be attributed to the province of Saurashtra of Gujarat and its centers like Sihor, Rajkot, Palitana and Bhavnagar as well. Tradition and practice of Peda making can be traced back to late 1800s in Sihor while it picking up momentum in 20th century. Along with Rajkot and Bhavnagar now, there are several distinct varieties of Peda, originating from different centers of Saurashtra. In Gujarat, Pedas are called and pronounced as Penda.

Recipe:

Ingredients:

- Khoya – ½ kg

- Ghee – 60 gm
- Powdered sugar – ½ kg
- Elaichi powder– 1/8 tsp or to taste

Method:

- Put the ghee and khoya in a pan and saute till brown.
- Mix in the elaichi powder and leave to cool.
- When cooled down, mix in the sugar till well blended.
- Form into desired sized rounds and serve.

LXXIV

Petha

Petha is a translucent soft candy from Agra. Usually rectangular or cylindrical, it is made from the ash gourd vegetable (also known as winter melon or white pumpkin, or simply petha in Hindi and Urdu). With growing demand and innovation, more varieties of the original preparation are available. Many flavoured variants are available, e.g. kesar petha, angoori petha etc. It is said that it originated in the royal kitchens of the Mughal Empirein Agra. The story goes that Emperor Shah Jahan once ordered his royal chefs to prepare a sweet that would be as pure and as white as the marble–clad Taj Mahal.It is said that during the 17th–century reign of Shah Jahan, this soft sugary sweet provided instant energy to the thousands of workers involved in building the Taj Mahal. The renowned petha from Agra known as *Pankshi peda* is almost 70 years old, who serves almost 20 types of pedas.

Recipe:

Ingredients:

- Ash gourd – 1 Kg
- Chemical lime – 1tsp
- Sugar – 1cup
- Water 1cup
- Thin milk – 2 tbsp
- Lemon juice – 1 tbsp
- Green cardamoms–peeled and crushed – 3–4 nos
- Gulab jal – 1 tsp

Method:

- Peel the pumpkin, remove the seeds and the soft, fibrous portion.
- Cut into large thick slices.
- Prick well with a fork all over.
- Dissolve 1 tsp of chemical lime in enough water to cover the pumpkin pieces.
- Soak them in this water and wash well. Cut into cubes.
- Make lime water solution with the remaining tsp of chemical lime.
- Soak the pumpkin pieces once more in the freshly made lime water for 2 hours.
- Drain pieces and wash thoroughly, squeezing out water and rinsing again so that no trace of lime remains.
- Boil enough water to take in the pumpkin pieces, add the pieces to it and cook till soft and transparent.
- Meanwhile, fill 3 cups of water and the sugar in a pan; place over low heat, stirring till sugar dissolves. Bring to a boil.
- Add the lemon juice and the cardamoms and cook till it reaches 'one thread' consistency.
- Skim off any foam that may collect along the sides of the pan.
- Keep the syrup warm.
- When the pumpkin pieces are cooked, drain with a slotted spoon and transfer into the syrup.
- Simmer for a couple minutes, take off stove and add the rose water and mix well.
- Cool and serve.

LXXV
Pitha

Pitha is a type of rice cake from the eastern regions of the Indian subcontinent, common in Bangladesh, Nepal and India, especially the eastern states of Bihar, Jharkhand, Kerala, Odisha, West Bengal and the Northeast India states, especially Assam. Pithas are typically made of rice flour, although there are some types of pitha made of wheat flour. Sweet pithas typically contain sugar, jaggery, date juice, or palm syrup, and can be filled with grated coconut, cashews, pistachios, sweetened vegetables, or fruits. Sweet pithas are also often flavored using cardamom or camphor. Depending on the type of pitha being prepared, pithas can be fried in oil or ghee, slow–roasted over a fire, steamed, or baked and rolled over a hot plate.Pithas are often eaten during breakfast, as a snack with (often with tea), and in dinner or lunch. Although there are many sweet varieties that are reserved for desserts or holidays.

Popular Variants of Pitha:

Gokul Pithe is a traditional dish that is made on the festival of Makar Sankranti or Poush Parbon in Bengali homes. These are sweet fried dumplings, soaked in thick hot sugar syrup. The filling is mostly of grated coconut and jaggery.

Kachi pitha– a pan baked pancake made from bora saul and filled with sesame seeds, ground coconut, dried orange rind, and jaggery.

Ghila pitha– a fried pitha made from bora saul and jaggery. Salt can also be used instead of jaggery for a savory variant.

Tekeli pitha– a special pitha made with both xaali saul and bora saul, mixed with coconut, sugar, and powdered milk. Ground cardamom and dried orange rind can also be added. The pitha is steamed in an earthenware pot set on a hearth.

Uhuwa pitha– Rice flour of Xaali Saul and Bora Saul is mixed with jaggery or salt and water and churned thoroughly. The paste is rolled into small balls and flattened and then boiled in water. It is served with tea and also can be eaten with milk.

Arisa Pitha –deep–fried pitha made from rice flour with jaggery or sugar.

Manda Pitha–steamed pitha made from rice flour, often with grated coconut and jaggery/sugar filling or fresh cheese (chhena) filling.

Kakara pitha–very popular fried pancake made from wheat flour/ semolina, often with a sweet coconut filling.

Recipe:

Ingredients:

- Grated coconut – 200 gms
- Khoya – 450 gms
- Sugar/date palm jaggery– ½ cup
- Flour – 150 gms
- Water – 5–6 cups
- Ghee – 40 gms
- Sodium bicarbonate – 1/8 tsp

Method:

- Make sugar syrup by heating 2 cups sugar with 4 cups of water.
- Allow it to cool. Fry the coconut, khoya and 2 tbsp of sugar together in a pan over medium flame. Stir it continuously.
- To make cakes, roll the mixture into balls and flatten between the palms.
- Make batter by mixing flour, remaining water, sodium bicarb and ghee.
- Heat ghee and coat coconut–milk cakes in the prepared batter.
- Deep fry until golden brown and immerse in the sugar syrup.

LXXVI
Pongal

Also called Sweet pongal is also known as Chakkara pongali in telugu and Sakkari pongal in tamil. It is made during Makara sankranti and also during other festivals. It is also offered to gods as a *Naivedyam*. This is the most common traditional recipe made with jaggery and no milk is used. Sweet pongal is known as Chakkara pongali in telugu & Sakkarai pongal in tamil. This dish is said to have been prepared by our ancestors to signify and celebrate – abundance and prosperity after the harvest. It is mostly made on Fridays or Tuesdays in Goddess Lakshmi and Durga temples as these are the special days the goddess is worshiped.It is called *huggi* in Kannada or in Karnataka.

Recipe:

Ingredients:

- Moong dal – 100 gm
- Powdered jaggery– 250 gm
- Spice cardamom – ¼ teaspoon
- Almonds – ¼ cup
- Coconut milk – 200 ml
- Rice – 100 gm
- Ghee – 200 gm
- Cashews – ¼ cup
- Raisins – ¼ cup
- Water – 300 ml

Method:

- First, take a non–stick pan and roast the rice and moong dal till they turn light golden yellow in colour.
- On another burner, put a pan over low flame and pour 100 ml water in it. Once it starts boiling, add jaggery powder to it. When the jaggery has dissolved and syrup is formed, put the burner down.
- In the meantime, cook rice and moong dal in the remaining water. Once half cooked, add coconut milk to it and cook further. Once rice and moong are almost cooked, add the jaggery syrup and sprinkle cardamom powder on it and put off the flame. Keep it aside.
- Now, put a pan on low flame and pour ghee in it. Let it melt and add cashews, almonds and raisins. Stir fry the dry fruits until they turn golden brown. Pour them over the rice mixture.
- Allow the dish to cook for about five minutes on low flame. Then, serve hot in small bowls.

LXXVII
Pootharekulu

Pootharekulu (plural) or poothareku (singular) is a popular Indian sweet from Atreyapuram, East Godavari, Andhra Pradesh, India. The sweet is wrapped in a wafer–thin rice starch layer resembling paper and is stuffed with sugar, dry fruits and nuts. It is made from a particular kind of rice batter called Jaya biyyam ('biyyam' meaning rice), combined with powdered sugar and ghee (clarified butter). Pootharekulu was consumed by the Kings and royal families on special occasions to celebrate joy and love. The tradition has been passed on from generation to generation and Pootharekulu is still used in weddings and special occasions in Andhra Pradesh to glorify the occasion. The name of the sweet literally means 'coated sheet' in the Telugu language—pootha means 'coating' and reku (plural rekulu) means 'sheet' in Telugu. The sweet has a history of a few centuries. It is said that a village woman first prepared the sweet by adding sugar and ghee to leftover rice starch. Atreyapuram villagers soon started making wrappers from rice flour, put sugar and ghee inside and folded them. They supply them to sweet manufacturers all over the two Telugu states. Pootharekulu can be stuffed with different fillings, including fine powdered sugar, jaggery, dry fruits, and chocolate powder. Hot and spicy pootharekulu are a relatively new variant.

Recipe:

Ingredients:

- Pootarekulu – 3 to 4 sheets
- Powdered Sugar – 1 cup
- Powdered jaggery– 1 cup

- Cardamom powder – 1 tsp
- Dry fruits –required amount
- Ghee –½ cup

Method:

- Dry roast cashews in a heavy bottom pan on a low to medium heat. Saute the cashews until light golden colour. Turn off the stove and transfer to other plate and allow them to cool completely. Grind into coarse powder and set aside.
- Grind sugar into fine powder and sift the powdered sugar without any lumps. when you are using jaggery shred the jaggery by using bigger slots of grater or grind it into fine powder. set aside.
- Add Cardamom powder into sugar or jaggery and mix it once completely or even add 2 to 3 cardamom pods while grinding along with sugar or jaggery. Set aside.
- Now into a large plate spread the wet cloth which is dipped and squeezed out all the water.
- Now take two layers of pootarekulu and place them on one side of the cloth as shown in the video and from the other side of the cloth cover the pootarekulu and pat it gently (do not pat it for longer time, poothareku may break), so by doing in this way the pootarekulu will soften and helps in folding without breaking.
- Now slowly take one end of the cloth as shown in the video, smear or sprinkle a spoon full of melted ghee to pootarekulu as shown in the video and by using tea strainer sprinkle a spoon full of sugar or required amount on poothareku, by doing this way sugar spreads evenly. When you sprinkle with fingers or with spoon sugar will not spread evenly. Sprinkle half tbsp cashew powder or required amount as shown in the video. [when you are using powdered jaggery instead of sugar, sprinkle 2 tbsp of shredded or powdered jaggery with fingers and sprinkle coarsely ground cashew powder].

- Now start folding the poothareku from one side halfway through and stop as the sheet is softened it will fold without breaking or crumbling into pieces and fold from the other side too as shown in the video.
- Now fold both edges of poothareku around 1 inch size and smear some ghee and you can even add powdered sugar of your choice. Now

fold from both the sides and make poothareku chutta as shown in the video.

- Now press it gently or evenly to flatten it or even you can place a plate on poothareku chutta.
- Transfer to other plate and do the remaining in the same procedure. After preparing each pootarekulu chutta rest them for 2 to 3 minutes on a plate and store in an air tight container.
- Serve poothareku chuttalu as a tea time snack or starter.

LXXVIII
Pukhlein

Pukhlein is a traditional rice flour bread recipe that owes its origin is Khasi hills in Meghalaya and is known for its palatable flavors all around the country. Making this sweet recipe is extremely easy and this dish will surely be a hit in your household. Breads are known for their fluffy texture and lightness that can be paired with almost any dish and that is why they are preferred by all. This regional recipe is made with the goodness of simple ingredients which are rice flour, cane sugar and refined oil and tastes absolutely divine. Made using fermented rice, cane sugar and oil, Pukhlein is a popular dessert, which is best paired with a hot cup of tea.

Recipe:

Ingredients:

- Rice flour–1cup
- Jaggery–½ cup
- Water –as required for melting the jiggery
- Oil – for deep frying

Method:

- In a pan dry roast rice flour on low flame for 5 minutes and keep aside.
- If you are using homemade rice flour, you can skip the above step.
- In a saucepan dissolve jaggery with water and cook to a thick syrup.
- Once the syrup is thick, slowly add the rice flour and mix well without any lumps.

- Cover the mixture with a wet cloth and keep aside.
- Now heat the oil in a pan for deep frying.
- With the mixture make small balls and press them with your palm into flat and deep fry in oil on medium flame until both sides turn into golden colour.
- Transfer them on to a kitchen towel to absorb excess oil.
- Repeat the process with the remaining mixture.
- Enjoy this tasty and crispy Pukhlein.

LXXIX
Rabri (Rabdi)

This is a sweet, condensed–milk–based dish, originating from the Indian subcontinent, made by boiling milk on low heat for a long time until it becomes dense and changes its colour to off–white or pale yellow. Jaggery, spices, and nuts are added to it to give it flavor. It is chilled and served as dessert. *Rabri* is the main ingredient in several desserts, such as *rasabali*, *chhena kheeri*, and *khira sagara*. A similar dish goes by the name *Basundi*. *Chandimangala* mentions *rabdi* (thickened, sweetened milk), along with other sweets in the early 1400s.

Recipe:

Ingredients:

- Full cream milk – 5 cups
- Sugar – ½ cup
- Green cardamoms – 4–5
- Blanched and shredded almonds – 12–15
- Blanched and shredded pistachios – 2 tbsp
- Vark leaves (silver leaves) – to decorate

Method:

- Boil the milk in a wide, heavy–based pan.
- Add the sugar and cardamom and simmer over low heat.
- Do not stir too often, as a layer of cream should form over it.
- After the layer is formed, push it away from the sides towards the centre, stir the milk below it gently to avoid scorching.

- Repeat the process till one–third of the volume of milk is left.
- The time taken will depend on the richness of the milk and the vessel.
- The wider the vessel and the richer the milk, the faster it will thicken.
- When done, the colour changes to a beige–cream, and the cream that was pushed aside, collects in layers.
- Remove from heat. When cool, transfer to a serving dish.
- Garnish with vark leaves (silver leaves) and nuts. Chill and serve.

LXXX
Rasabali

Rasabali is a sweet dish from Odisha, India. Rasabali is offered to Baladev, and originated in the Baladevjew Temple of Kendrapara. It is one of the Chapana bhoga of Jagannath temple.

It consists of deep fried flattened reddish brown patties of chhena (farmer cheese) that are soaked in thickened, sweetened milk (rabri). Flattening the chhena into palm–sized patties is done in order to allow them to absorb the milk more readily. The thickened milk is also usually lightly seasoned with crushed cardamoms.

Recipe:

Ingredients:

- Full cream Milk – 1 litre
- Vinegar – 2 tsps
- Cardamom powder – ¼ tsp
- Semolina – 1 tsp
- Wheat flour – 1 tsp
- Sugar – 3 tbsp
- oil – for frying
- Kewra water – 2 – 3 drops
- Sliced Almonds and Pistachios – 1 tbsp
- Silver varq and Tulsi leaves – for garnish

Method:

- Warm 500 ml milk, once it comes to boiling point add vinegar and switch off the flame. Immediately the milk will start curdling.
- In muslin cloth drain the water and hang the chenna for an hour so that the water drains out completely. To get rid of vinegar smell you can cold bath the tied chenna once or twice before hanging it.
- In the meantime start boiling another 500 ml milk adding sugar to it till it reduced to almost half of the original quantity. Add cardamom powder and mix. Remove from heat.
- Now take the chenna, semolina, wheat flour and knead it smoothly for 3 to 5 minute. Now divide into 7 equal sized ball ,flatten each ball on your palm into a circular tikki shape.
- Heat oil and deep fry them. Add fried cottage cheese into thick milk. Add sliced almonds and pistachios.
- Garnish with silver varq and Tulsi leaves. Let it cool completely. Serve with love.

LXXXI

Rasgulla

Rasgulla is an Indian syrupy dessert popular in the India. It is made from ball–shaped dumplings of chhena (an Indian cottage cheese) and semolina dough, cooked in light syrup made of sugar. This is done until the syrup permeates the dumplings. The dish originated in East India; the present–day states of Odisha and West Bengal have variously claimed to be its birthplace and both of them been accorded th GI tag. Rasgulla is derived from the words *ras* ("juice") and *gulla* ("ball"). According to historians of Odisha, the rasgulla originated in Puri, as *Kheer Mohan*, which later evolved into the Pahala rasgulla. It has been traditionally offered as bhog to goddess Lakshmi at Jagannath Temple, Puri. Another theory claims that the spongy white rasgulla is believed to have been introduced in present–day West Bengal in 1868 by a Kolkata–based confectioner named Nobin Chandra Das in his sweet shop located at Sutanuti (present–day Baghbazar). Another account states that that a man named Braja Moira had introduced rasgulla in his shop near Calcutta High Court in 1866, two years before Das started selling the dish. In 1930, the *Rasgulla* was canned and exported to different countries by KC Das and gained popularity across the globe.

Recipe:

Ingredients:

For chenna / paneer–

- Full cream cow's milk – 1 litre
- Lemon juice – 2 tbsp
- Water – 1 cup **For sugar syrup–**
- Sugar – 1½ cup

- Water – 8 cups

Method:

Chenna / paneer Recipe:

- Firstly, in a thick bottomed pan add 1 litre milk.
- Furthermore, stir occasionally and get to a boil.
- Additionally, add lemon juice and stir well.
- Add more lemon juice and stir till milk curdles completely.
- And immediately drain the curdled milk into the hand kerchief.
- Pour a cup of water and clean the paneer as it has lemon juice in it.
- Furthermore, bring it together and squeeze off excess water.
- Hang for 30 minutes. Or till all the water drains off completely.
- After 30 minutes, start to knead the paneer.
- Knead paneer till it turns out smooth without any grains of milk.
- Furthermore, make small balls of paneer and keep aside.

Sugar syrup Recipe:

- Firstly, in a deep vessel take 1½ cup of sugar.
- Furthermore, add 8 glasses of water and stir well.
- Boil the syrup for 10 minutes on medium flame.
- After that, drop the prepared paneer balls into boiling sugar syrup.
- Cover and boil for 15 minutes. The paneer balls will have doubled in size.
- Furthermore, keep aside till it cools completely and then refrigerate.
- Finally, serve rasgulla chilled or at room temperature garnished with few saffron strands.

LXXXII

Ras Kadam

Ras kadam is also known as Kheer kadam/ Khoya kodom/ Kheer kodom and it is very famous sweet dish recipe of India, especially Tripura, Jharkhand, West Bengal and Odisha. A traditional recipe made with the enticing combination of khoya, milk, red edible colour, green cardamom powder and sugar giving it a shape of a fruit known as Kadam (*Burflower*). The addition of saffron elevates the flavours of this delectable dish and brings a wave of sweet flavours in your mouth. This sweet can be served in all occasions.

Recipe:

Ingredients:

- Milk – ½ liter
- White vinegar – 1tbsp
- Khoya (Dried Whole Milk) – 1 cup
- Poppy Seeds – 4 tbsp
- Desiccated coconut Powder – 4 tbsp
- Dry Milk Powder – 4 tbsp
- Cardamom Powder – 1 tbsp
- Mixture of Sugar and Jaggery – 1 cup

Method:

- Boil milk in a pot and add vinegar for making cream cheese.
- Discard excess water from cream cheese and Wrap the cotton cloth and form a solid structure

- With the help of hand mash it for 5 to 10 minutes and make equal bolls of 1‖ diameter size
- Prepare syrup of sugar and jaggery along with cardamom powder and put the bolls and cook it for 15 to 20 minutes.
- Let it stay in the syrup for 3 hours and after that discard the syrup.
- For preparing outer cover take khoya and mash it for 5 to 10 minutes add 2 tbsp. sugar.
- Take khoya and prepare the outer surface and place bolls in between.
- Cover it and dust with your desired dusting.
- Refrigerate it for 15 minutes and your recipe is ready to be served.

LXXXIII
Ras Malai

Ras malai or Rossomalai is a heavenly dessert originating from the eastern regions of the Indian subcontinent, possibly Bengal or Odisha. The name *ras malai* is the Hindi cognate of Bengali– *rosh*, meaning "juice", and *molai*, meaning "cream". It has been described as "a rich cheesecake without a crust".The sweet is of Bengali origin; according to K.C. Das Grandsons, it was invented by K.C. Das. Rasmalai undoubtedly tops the list of all Indian milk based desserts. This scrumptious dessert is quite popular in Indian households and is made during various festivals and special occasions.

Recipe:

Ingredients:

- Full cream cow's milk – 1 litre
- Lemon juice – 2 tbsp
- Water – 1 cup

For sugar syrup–

- Sugar – 1½ cup
- Water – 8 cups

For rabri / rabdi–

- Full cream milk –1 litre
- Sugar–¼ cup
- Cardamom powder–½ tsp

- Saffron milk–2 tbsp
- Chopped pistachios–7 nos.
- Chopped almonds–5 nos.
- Choppedcashews – 10nos.

Method:

Chenna / paneer Recipe:

- Firstly, boil milk.
- Additionally, add lemon juice and stir till milk curdles completely.
- Drain the curdled milk and squeeze off excess water.
- After 30 minutes, start to knead the paneer for 10 minutes.
- Furthermore, make small balls and flatten. Keep aside.

Sugar syrup Recipe:

- Firstly, take sugar and water.
- Boil the syrup for 10 minutes.
- After that, drop the prepared paneer balls.
- Cover and boil for 15 minutes.
- Furthermore, squeeze of sugar syrup.

Rabri / rabdi Recipe:

- Firstly, heat milk and get to a boil.
- Once a layer of cream is formed over the milk, stick it to sides of vessel.
- Repeat the process for at least 5 times or till milk reduces to one–third.
- Further, add sugar, cardamom powder and saffron milk.
- Give a good mix and get to boil.
- Also scrape off the collected cream from sides. And give a good stir.
- Further, refrigerate for 2–3 hours.

Service–

- Firstly, pour the chilled rabri / rabdi over the squeezed paneer balls.
- Finally garnish with few chopped nuts and allow to absorb for 2 hours.

LXXXIV
Rotana

Roat is very popular sweet bread that is made in the Northern regions of Uttarakhand. It's especially made for wedding functions and festivals. As a sign of celebration, this bread is made in large numbers and served to the friends and relatives of the wedding party. It is also popular in Hyderabad. Roat is subtly flavoured with some crushed fennel seeds, cardamom and jaggery that gives it sweetness and is similar to Roat of Hyderabad, which is more like cookie. This mix of flavours is what gives this popular bread a rather unique taste. Traditionally, this flat bread is made for Hanumanji's festival – *Jhandi* and in Hyderabad, it is made during Muharam.

Recipe:

Ingredients:

- Plain flour – ½ cups
- Caster sugar – ½ cup
- Gr.cardamom powder – 1 tsp
- Ghee (room temperature, slurry like consistency) – 100 ml
- Milk (approximately, at room temperature) – 1 cup
- Extra ghee – for frying

Method:

- Add sugar and cardamom to flour.
- Mix in ghee with your fingers.
- Add milk gradually, to form a soft, scone – like dough. You may need more or less, so don't pour all at one go.

- Divide dough into ten balls and flatten into discs, about 3 mm thick. You may have to use a rolling pin for this.
- Heat ghee on a medium flame. Fry roat on the medium flame till golden brown on both sides. (Be careful, frying at too high a temperature will cause the roat to be raw inside).

LXXXV

Sael Roti

Sel roti is a traditional homemade, sweet, ring–shaped rice bread/doughnut originating from the Indian subcontinent. It is mostly prepared during Dashain and Tihar, widely celebrated Hindu festivals in Nepal and Sikkim and Darjeeling regions in India. Sel roti are cooked in bulk and can be stored at room temperature for least 20 days. Sel roti are often sent as special gifts to family members living away from home or used as prasad in puja. The first iteration of this fermented bread, which gets its name from the rice variety Sel, which grows in the foothills of Himalayas. Old tales say that the concept of Sel Roti came from the Babari, an original —roti‖ that was more of a pancake. Sel–Roti resembles a large thin puffed–up doughnut and has a crispy texture with reddish brown color. It is prepared by grinding soaked rice to create a thick batter. It is then mixed with sugar, clarified butter, mashed banana, water, poured into bubbling oil and deep–fried.

Recipe:

Ingredients:

- Rice – 1 kg
- Water or milk–500 ml
- Ghee–2 cups
- Sugar –2 cups
- Cooking Oil– liter

Method:

- Wash and soak rice overnight, drain excess water.

- Mix ghee and sugar and grind into fine paste. The paste should be fine and greasy.
- Continuously stir the mixture.
- Cover it and leave at the room temperature for 1–2 hours to melt and mix all the ingredients
- Heat pan with cooking oil. The pan should be deep enough to float sel and the base should be flat.
- Watch for vapor/smoke from the oil or see the picking stick float on the oil.
- Pour the not too thick batter as continuous ring into hot oil till they become brown/golden.
- Confirm both sides are brown.

LXXXVI
Sandesh

Sandesh or Shondesh is a dessert, originating in 16th century from the Bengal region in the eastern part of the Indian subcontinent, created with milk and sugar. Sondesh is derived from Hindi word 'Sandesh' which means news or message. Bengalis practiced this tradition of sending sweets or food as a gift to families and friends and hence the sweet got its name. One can find a sweet dish named Sandesh in the Medieval Bengali Literature. The older version of this sweet dish was prepared by solidified kheer. The Portuguese influence resulted into the modern chenna based Sandesh. It is said that the extreme heat of Calcutta summer began to rot *Chhana*. To counter this daily wastage of tasteless but useful by product of milk it was mixed with the molasses or sugar and a fine paste was made out of it. A great mind started mixing sugar, *khoya* and cardamom powder with it and it finally resulted in beautiful and awesome tasting paste known as *makha sandesh*. That was the first form of the *sandesh*, known to Bengalis.

Recipe:

Ingredients:

- Milk – 8 cups
- Castor Sugar – ½ cup
- Lemon juice – ¼ cup
- Green cardamom powder – as required
- Pistachios blanched and chopped – 12 nos.

Method:

- Bring the milk to a boil in a deep, thick–bottomed non–stick pan. Add the lemon juice and stir till the milk curdles. Strain and immediately refresh the chhenna in chilled water.
- Put the chhenna in a piece of muslin and squeeze till all the water is drained out.
- Knead the chhenna well with the heel of your hand. Add caster sugar and cardamom powder, and knead again.
- Cook in a non–stick pan on medium heat for eight minutes. Remove from heat and divide into twelve equal portions. Roll each portion into a ball and make a dent on the top.
- When cooled, place a pistachio in the dent and serve. Makes 12 sandesh/350 gms.

LXXXVII
Shahi Tukra

Shahi Tukra as the name suggests means royal dessert which is an exotic rich bread pudding is eaten in Pakistan and India, and it's particularly famous in Delhi, Lucknow. In North India and Pakistan, where it's made of bread deep–fried in ghee, soaked in sugar syrup, and then piled high with rabri and dried fruit, cardamom and nuts, it's called Shahi tukda, meaning *"Royal piece"*. It's a simple recipe to make and an exceptional dessert for times when you are in a hurry. Shahi Tukra or Shahi tukray or Shahi Tukda are almost similar method of cooking with slight variations and are originally Mughlai desserts from the Nawabi cuisine. Considered a part of Mughlai and Awadhi North Indian aristocratic cuisines, Shahi tukda's origins are mysterious. Some say that Babur, the founder of the Mughal dynasty, brought it with him to South Asia in the 16th century, and that it descends from Middle Eastern bread puddings such as *eish es serny* and the Egyptian *um ali*. Others claim the sweet is actually a Mughal take on the bread pudding brought by British East India company officers in the 17th century. While it may have originally been made with roti or even with fried clotted cream, shahi tukda is now mostly made with sliced packaged English bread, demonstrating the culinary creativity with which South Asian people responded to colonialism.

Recipe:

Ingredients:

- Bread slice – 4
- Sugar – 1 cup (200 gms.) (For sugar syrup)
- Milk – 500 ml

- Sugar –2tbsp (for rabdi)
- Saffron – 20 to 25 threads
- Green cardamom – 4 (peel and ground coarsely)
- Chironji – 1 tbsp
- Almonds – 4 (thinly sliced)
- Pistachios – 8 to 10 (thinly sliced)
- Desi ghee – ½ cup (100 gms.)

Method:

- Take sugar in any vessel. Add ½ cup water into it and place it on flame for cooking syrup.
- After it simmers once and sugar dissolves completely, prepare sugar syrup with one thread consistency.
- Take milk in any other vessel with heavy bottom and place it on flame for heating.
- Allow the milk to simmer on medium flame and cook until milk remains ¼ from the whole quantity.
- Turn off the flame now and mix the malai collected at the corner of the vessel. Also add sugar, cardamom powder and rabdi is ready.
- For making shahi tukda, cut the bread into two halves, diagonally or in rectangular shape as per your preference.
- Heat some ghee in a wok. When ghee is medium hot, place 2 to 3 bread slices into it and fry until they golden brown in color. Similarly fry all bread slices.
- Soak each fried bread slice in sugar syrup for 10 to 15 seconds and then take them out and place on a plate. Dip all the bread slices in sugar syrup.
- Place the sugar syrup coated bread slices in a plate one by one and spread 1 to 2 tsp rabdi over each bread slice.
- Sprinkle some dry fruits, chironji, saffron thread to garnish.
- Scrumptious shahi tukda is ready, serve and relish eating.
- Shahi tukda can be stored in refrigerator for up to 2 days.

LXXXVIII

Shankarpali (Shakkarpara)

Shankarpali is an Indian snack popular in Western India, especially in Gujarat, Maharashtra and Karnataka. It is traditionally enjoyed as a treat on Diwali. It is rich in carbohydrates, making it an instant source of energy. It can be sweet, sour or spicy depending upon how it is made. In Gujarati it is called Shakkarpara, in Marathi it is called Shankarpali, in Bengali it is called Shakerpara, in Urdu/Hindi it is called Shakarpare.

Recipe:

Ingredients:

- Refined flour / maida – 500 gms
- Semolina –250 gms
- Milk– 3/4th cup to 1 cup
- Sugar –300 gms
- Ghee – ½ cup
- Salt – a pinch
- Oil – as required for frying

Method:

- Make a small Pan heat the Vanaspati ghee/ ghee and keep aside.
- Now sift flour, then add semolina, powdered sugar and salt. Put warm dalda / ghee. Rub the dalda with the flour through your finger. It should

appear like bread crumbs.

- Time to add milk. Start kneading to form soft and smooth dough.
- Keep kneading the dough for about 15 to 20 mins with pressure.
- Keep the dough aside covered with a damp cotton cloth for about 10 to 15 mins. It's time now to make big balls out of the dough and roll them with the chapati roller.
- Roll them into round shape similar to a roti but keep the width about ½ inches. Take a knife and cut them into square shape.
- Now make vertical and horizontal lines each measuring more than an inch square. Alternatively you could cut them into diamond shape.
- Heat oil in a kadhai once the oil is hot, add the Shankarpali to it ensuring gas is on low flame. Once the Shankarpali are nice golden brown remove them. Repeat the same procedure with the remaining of the dough.

LXXXIX

Sheer Khurma

Sheer khurma, also known as sheer korma, is a special dish made with dates, milk and sewai or vermicelli. *Khurma* means dates in Urdu. This special dish is served after Eid prayer as breakfast and throughout the day to all visiting guests. The dish is vastly popular in Hyderabad, where it is consumed first thing in the morning. The garnish on sheer khurma includes dried dates, also known as *chhuara* and coconut along with nuts like almonds, cashew nuts and pistachios.This dish is made from various dry fruits, vermicelli, thickened milk, sugar etc. Depending on the region, cardamom, pistachios, almonds, cloves, saffron, raisins, and rose water are also added.

Recipe:

Ingredients:

- Full cream Milk–500 ml
- Roasted vermicelli –50 gms
- Sugar– ¼ cup
- Chopped dates – 1tbsp
- Raisins– ¼ cup
- Blanched and sliced almonds – ¼ cup
- Pistachios– ¼ cup
- Ghee– ¼ cup
- Saffron– ½ tsp
- Cardamom powder– ½ tsp

Method:

- Take a pan and pour ghee in it.
- Add almonds, raisins and pistachios to it. Saute well.
- Now in another hot pan with ghee, add vermicelli. Roast well.
- In another wide pan simmer the milk till it thickens, add sugar and simmer again.
- Add the roasted vermicelli and dry fruits along with dates and saffron.
- Mix well till simmer. Add cardamom powder. Bring to simmer.
- Serve chilled, garnished with dates.

XC
Shor Bhaja

Shor Bhaja or Sar Bhajais a delicacy made of milk cream along with other ingredients. It is purely made of cream of the milk. Sometimes khoya and chhanna are also mixed with it. It follows one of the most difficult and tedious processes of making sweets. It needs extreme patience and expert skills. Krishnanagar (Nadia, West Bengal) is also known as the birthplace of this sweet and many renowned sweet confectioneries in Kolkata make these Shor Bhaja during festival times only.

Recipe:

Ingredients:

- Full cream milk – 3 liters
- Sugar – 3 cups
- Water – 4 cups
- Cardamom powder – 1 tbsp
- Rose essence – 1 drop
- Vegetable oil – 1½ – 2 cups
- Caster sugar – 1 tbsp (I couldn't find them handy so I used normal sugar)
- All – purpose flour – ½ tsp (if required)
- Lemon – 1/6thof a regular lemon
- Pistachioslivers – for decoration
- Khoya/ milk powder – 1 tsp for decoration

Method:

- Boil the milk on high flame.
- Turn the flame to simmer once cream starts forming on top of the milk. Wait for few minutes. Let the cream settle on the top of the milk. Then again turn the flame to high. Don't stir the milk while boiling as our aim is to collect the cream form the top of the milk.
- Continue the process until the cream is thick enough to scoop out.
- Take a long spatula and start from one side of the pan and start pushing the thick layer of cream towards the exact opposite direction.
- Make it real slow so that the cream layer doesn't get disturbed.
- Push it further when you reach the body of the pan.
- Now push it upwards and try to stick it to the body of the pan. This step is extremely difficult and hectic too. If you break the cream it will melt in the milk and will turn it thicker. And you need to start from scratch again.
- Now push it upwards and try to stick it to the body of the pan. This step is extremely difficult and hectic too. If you break the cream it will melt in the milk and will turn it thicker. And you need to start from scratch again.
- Scoop off the cream when it is at least ¼th inch. thick. And place it on a large flat palate. Continue the process until you are done with the entire milk.
- Now arrange the layers of the cream on the palate evenly. Make sure there is no milk at all in the cream. If there is any milk squeeze it out by pressing the layers gently. The layer of cream should be dry but moist.
- Sprinkle some caster sugar on the top or between the layers.
- If you find your cream layer is still a bit watery sprinkle some all – purpose flour on the top of the layer and distribute it evenly.
- Leave it for few minutes to absorb the liquid.
- By pressing the top make the layer even and as smoother as possible.
- Now run a knife roughly to make square pieces out of it.
- Now heat oil in a nonstick wok on medium flame. Take a square at a time. Reshape it with the flat knife or spatula and add them in the oil slowly.
- Add 3 – 4 pieces at a time.
- Make sure all pieces are separated.
- Fry them on medium – high flame until they are golden brown in color.
- Turn the cakes upside down once to fry the reverse side as well. Fry them until they are brown in color on the both sides.

- In mean while add water in a deep bottomed vessel and let it boil on high flame. Once bubbles start appearing add sugar and stir continuously until sugar is dissolved.
- Add cardamom powder and essence and give it a light stir. Keep boiling.
- Squeeze 1/6th of a lemon to extract the juice. Add 3 – 4 drops of this juice into the syrup. Once you are done with the frying, remove them with a slotted spoon and dunk them directly into the sugar syrup. Let it boil on medium flame.
- Keep the syrup boiling for 10 –15 mins more or until you notice the sugar syrup getting thicker.
- Now use the back of a spatula to poke a Shor bhaja. If it gets back to its shape you are done.
- Remove the pan from fire and let it cool.
- Decorate with some sliver of pistachio and sprinkle some khoya on the top.
- Serve it hot or cold.

XCI
Shrikhand

Shrikhand is an Indian sweet dish made of strained dahi (yogurt). Shrikhand has been referred to as "*Shikhrini*" in the Sanskrit literature. According to Jashbhai B. Prajappati and Baboo M. Nair, it originated in ancient Indian state Maharashtra, around 400 B.C.E.

The exact origin of Shrikhand is unknown but Western India is credited with the first historical mention of the dish. Its origin may be traced from Mahabharata where there are tales that Bhim invented this recipe and named it after Shri Krishna i.e. Shrikhanda. Another set of opinion say that Shrikhand was invented in *Mudpaak Khana* of Bajirao Peshwa. Hence it is a very popular dessert in Maharashtra and Gujarat. The dish is very popular in Gujarat and Rajasthan but other states like Maharashtra and Punjab do have local variations that are popular too. Although there is no exact record of how the dish came about, the legend states that traveling herdsmen hung curd or yoghurt overnight to make it easier to carry while traveling. The thick yoghurt that was collected the next day was mixed with sugar and nuts to make it palatable during the long journey. Mango tinged shrikhand is called *Amarkhand*.

Recipe:

Ingredients:

- Curd / yogurt, thick and fresh – 2 cups
- Powdered sugar – ¼ cup
- Saffron water – 2 tbsp
- Cardamom powder – ¼ tsp
- Chopped almonds – 1 tsp

- Chopped pistachios – 1 tsp

Method:

- Firstly, place a sieve in a large mixing bowl. Make sure there is enough space for water to accumulate at the bottom of the bowl without touching the sieve.
- Further place a cheese cloth or a hand kerchief into the bowl.
- Pour 2 cups of fresh – thick curd.
- Get the cloth together and tie it tightly.
- Furthermore, refrigerate it overnight. Make sure to refrigerate else the curd will turn sour and need to add more sugar.
- The next day, we can see the water has separated from the curd.
- Thick and creamy curd is ready which is also known as hung curd.
- Further, add in powdered sugar.
- Also add saffron water. To prepare saffron water, soak few strands of saffron in 2 tbsp of hot water.
- Mix well making sure the sugar gets dissolved in curd.
- Further add cardamom powder and again give a quick mix.
- Transfer to the piping bag or directly scoop into a serving bowl.
- Furthemore, squeeze the piping bag into the serving bowl.
- Also garnish with few chopped almonds and pistachios.
- Finally, store in refrigerator or serve immediately.

XCII
Shufta

Shufta is a traditional Kashmiri dessert especially made during festivals and Marriages. It is a mixture of various dry fruits and spices, like (black pepper powder, dry ginger powder, cinnamon powder and cardamom powder) coated with sugar syrup. Although Kashmiri Shufta looks very simple, it tastes awesome. Dry fruits are first soaked in water for some time and then mixed with ghee and fried, Coated with various spice powders and sugar.

Recipe:

Ingredients:

- Cottage cheese paneer cut into cubes – ½ cup
- Ghee – ½ cup
- Almond – ½ cup
- Cashew nuts – ½ cup
- Big raisins– ½ cup
- Pistachio – ½ cup
- Dry coconut slices – ½ cup
- Sugar – 2 cups
- Cinnamon powder – 1tsp
- Black pepper powder – 1tsp
- Dry ginger powder – 1tsp
- Cardamom powder – 1tsp
- Saffron dissolved in water – 1tsp
- Rose essence – few drops
- Chopped dry dates – 8–10

Method:

- Soak all the nuts and raisins in water for half an hour.
- Soak dry dates in luke warm water and chop them into small pieces.
- Heat ghee in a heavy bottomed pan heat ghee and fry coconut slices till brown.
- Fry paneer pieces till slightly brown in the same ghee.
- Make sugar syrup by heating the sugar in 1 cup of water.
- Drain the dry fruits and add them in the pan. Add the sugar syrup, coconut slices and all the spices to this. Cook till sugar thickens.
- Garnish with silver leaf and serve.

XCIII
Sithabhog

Sitabhog is a famous sweet of Bardhaman, West Bengal, India. Sitabhog is a flavourful dessert that looks like white rice or vermicelli mixed with small pieces of Gulab jamun called *Nikhuti*. Made from cottage cheese (also known as chhana in Bengali), rice flour and sugar, Sitabhog often gives the appearance of pulao, which is albeit sweet in taste.

According to Late Nagendranath Nag, his grandfather Late Khettranath Nag first invented special Sitabhog in Bardhaman during the regime of Maharaja Late Mahatabchand Bahadur. Seventy two years after this invention the name of Sitabhog earned its reputation all over India after the arrival of Lord Curzon in Bardhaman and his appraisal for these two sweets.

On invitation of Maharaja Vijaychand Mahatab Lord Curzon visited Bardhaman on 19 August 1904. To memorize the welcome lunch of Lord Curzon, Maharaja ordered Vairabchandra Nag, a sweet – maker of the town, to prepare something new and unique which would amaze the Lord. Vairabchandra Nag undertook the responsibility and introduced two new preparations named Sitabhog. Lord Curzon was surprised to have such unique sweets and praised and thanked Vairabchandra Nag in the certificate given to him saying he never had such sweet ever before. Thereafter, the quality and name of these two sweets reached all over the country and abroad. Late Nagendranath Nag, son of Late Vairabchandra Nag, broadcast this incident on Radio on 15 November 1976.

Recipe:

Ingredients:

- Basmati rice – 1 cup

- Crumbled Paneer – 1 cup
- Cardamom Powder – 1tsp
- Raisins – 1tbsp
- Pistachios – 1tbsp
- Saffron strands – Few
- Sugar – 1 cup
- Ghee or oil – for frying

Ingredients for Nikhuti (jamuns)

- Milk Powder – 1 cup
- Maida – ½ cup
- Cooking soda – 1/4 tsp
- Ghee – 1 tbsp
- Curd – 2 tbsp
- Sugar – 1 cup
- Cardamom Powder – 1 tsp

Method:

- To begin making the Bengali Sita Bhog, we will first make a rice and chhena vermicelli. You can either use a wide holed grater or a sev maker to make the vermicelli. This fried vermicelli will then be soaked in sugar syrup.
- Soak 1 cup of the Basmati rice in water for 1 to 2 hours. After a couple of hours, drain the water and spread the rice over a kitchen towel and allow it to dry.
- Once dry place the rice in a dry grinder and grind to a fine powder.
- Add the rice powder and chenna to a large mixing bowl. Knead both of them together adding little milk at a time to make soft, firm and smooth dough. Cover and allow the dough to rest for a few minutes till we get the sugar syrup ready.
- For the sugar syrup, place the sugar along with 1 cup of water and bring it to a boil. Once the sugar comes to a boil, turn the heat to low and simmer to make sticky syrup. When you touch the syrup between your fingers, it should feel sticky and slightly stringy.
- Once the sugar syrup is ready, add the cardamom powder and the saffron to it and allow it to rest.

- We will now deep fry the rice mixture by making it either into oblong shape by running it through a grater or a sev maker. The size of the rice vermicelli is purely your preference.
- Heat oil for deep frying. Once the oil is heated, place the rice and chenna mixture through a grater and grate it into the hot oil. You will notice small rice size bits drop out into the oil. Deep fry on medium heat till the Bhog turns golden brown in color.
- Drain out the excess oil and proceed the same way with the remaining rice mixture. Add the raisins and the fried rice and chenna into the sugar syrup. Allow it to soak well in the syrup for about 10 to 15 minutes. You will notice the rice and chenna vermicelli starts to puff up and turn soft.
- Once it is soaked, spread it on a plate and allow the grains of sugar coated rice to cool.
- In the next step we will make the Nikhuti (the jamun balls).
- In a large mixing bowl add milk powder, maida, soda, ghee and yogurt and mix them all together. Add little water at a time and knead to make a firm and smooth dough. Allow the dough to test for about 5 to 10 minutes.
- After 10 minutes, shape them into small tiny jamuns (balls).
- In the same oil we deep fried the rice vermicelli, heat that oil and add a few jamuns at a time and deep fry until golden brown in color. Once fried, keep them aside.
- The next step is to soak these jamuns in sugar syrup. To make the sugar syrup in another pan add water and sugar and bring it to boil.
- Once it comes to a boil, turn the heat to medium and make light syrup. This syrup does not have to be very sticky. Once the syrup is ready, place the small jamun balls into the hot syrup and allow it to soak and become soft. These Nikhutis will puff up a little.
- Once soaked drain from the syrup and add it to the rice vermicelli we made.
- Transfer it to a serving bowl, garnish it with pistachios and serve

XCIV
Singori

Singori (also spelled Singodi) or Singauri is an Indian sweet of Kumaon region made with Khoya and wrapped in maalu leaf. It is similar to *Kalakhand*. According to some historians the origin of Singori is believed to be the old province of Almora.

Recipe:

Ingredients:

- Unsweetened khoya – ¼ gms.
- Fresh grated coconut – 100 gms.
- Sugar – ¼ gms.
- Maalu leafs – 16 nos.
- Rose petals – for garnish
- Nuts – 20 gms

Method:

- Take a deep bowl, add khoya on it and knead it by adding sugar on it .
- Heat the mixture of khoya and sugar till khoya melts.
- Add grated coconut and continued heating for 8 minutes on low medium flame.
- As mixture cools down, fill small khoya balls in each maalu cone shaped leafs.
- Garnish it with rose petals or nuts.

XCV
Sohan Halwa

Sohan halwa is a traditional dessert that is made with milk, sugar, water, corn flour, ghee and lots of dry fruits. Unlike most halwas, it is solid and is in a disc–like shape. It is also called *Gheewala halwa* since the Mughal era. The Hafiz Halwa shop in Multan claims it was introduced by Dewan Sawan Mal, the ruler of Multan in 1750. However, there is a theory that it was invented in Persia by Iranian people and it was considered an ancient sweet served during social gatherings. S. Abdul Khaliq claims that this halwa was introduced in the Indian subcontinent in the early 16th century during the reign of Mughal emperor Humayun. This Halwa is famous allover northern India and is generally served Moharram and in elite class family gatherings.

Recipe:

Ingredients:

- Sugar– ½ kg
- Cornflour or maida – ½ kg
- Almonds– ¼ kg
- Pistachio – 100 gm
- Green cardamom – 50 gm
- Ghee – ½ kg
- Milk – 1 cup
- Water – 2 liters
- Saffron – 1 tsp

Method:

- Heat 1 liter water, add sugar and boil for 5 minutes.
- Add 1 cup milk and boil for 5 minutes.
- Strain it through a muslin bag or thin cloth.
- Add the remaining water and sugar syrup.
- Dissolve 1 tsp saffron in warm water and add.
- Dissolve the cornflour in a little water. Add to the cornflour mixture and cook over low flame.
- When cornflour becomes thick, add 1 tbsp ghee.
- Continue adding ghee (½ kg) slowly during cooking to prevent it from sticking to the pan.
- Stir it well. As ghee separates from the mixture, then it is ready.
- Add almonds, pistachio & green cardamoms in it.
- Grease a pan or tray with oil.
- Spread halwa in it & press with a wooden spoon to flatten it.
- Garnish it with almonds, pistachio and cardamoms.
- As it cools down, cut it into pieces and serve.

XCVI

Sutarfeni

Sutarfeni is a sweet Rajasthani and Gujrati treat consisting of rice flour that is roasted in ghee and combined with melted sugar to develop a structure similar to cotton candy. The sweet is usually flavored with cardamom and topped with nuts such as almonds and pistachios. Its texture is described in the name – *sutar* means *thread*, and *feni* means *fine*. Vijayanagar records indicate that Pheni was another much relished sweet dish prepared from wheat flour and sugar.

Recipe:

Ingredients:

- Feni strands – 100 gm
- Sugar – 4 cups
- Water– 2 cups Coarsly Ground Powder
- Pistachios – 5 nos
- Saffron – 5 strands
- Almonds – 3 nos
- Gr.cardamom pdr. – ½ tsp

Method:

- Make 1–strand sugar syrup. Let it cool completely for a few hours.
- Take the feni strands and cover it with a damp cloth or paper towel.
- Take a few strands at a time and twirl it into a small circle.
- You can arrange them on a tray and cover with a damp cloth.
- Place the twirled feni strands in a deep spoon with holes.

- Deep–fry for 30 seconds (please make sure it does not brown).
- Remove the fried circles and stack them up in piles.
- Using your hand, take each circle and dip thoroughly in the sugar syrup.
- Hold it above the container for a minute and let it drain completely.
- Place them in the container that you are going to store it in.
- Sprinkle the pistachio powder over the Sutarfeni.

XCVII

Thekua

Thekua or Khajuria or *Thokwa* or Thikari is a dry sweet from the Indian subcontinent. It is very popular in Bihar, Jharkhand, Bengal, Eastern Uttar Pradesh (Purvanchal) and Terai region of Nepal. It is a mandatory item during the festivals of Teej, Jitiya, Chhat Puja and wedding ceremonies.Thekua is traditionally made of whole wheat flour, raisins, dry coconut, jaggery or sugar and ghee or refined oil. First of all, a solution of sugar or jaggery is made with water. This is then added to the wheat flour to form dough. This is followed by rolling a small chunk of the dough and pressing it against the wooden mould that has been greased with ghee. The flattened piece is then deep – fried in the oil or ghee till golden brown.

Recipe:

Ingredients:

- Maida – 500gms.
- Suji – 500gms.
- Sugar – 500gms.
- Milk – 250gms.
- Ghee – 100gms.
- Chhuhara – 50gms.
- Elaichi powder – 20gms.
- Dry coconut – 50gms.
- Raisins (kismis) – 50gms.
- Saunf – 20gms.
- Ghee for deep frying – 500gms

Method:

- Cut all the dry fruits into very small pieces.
- Mix all the items including milk and ghee in a bowl and spray water in small Amount. Mixture should be a little hard. (mixture should not stick to your hands.)
- Make pieces off the size off cookies with your hand.
- Put a pan on the gas stove. Put ghee in it. Let it be heated for some time.
- Deep fry the cookies until they turn brownish in color.
- Take out the cookies from the pan. Now your snack is ready.

XCVIII

Unni Appam

Unniappam is a delicious and sweet snack from Kerala. Unni appam, also called *Karollappam* is a small round fritters made from rice, jaggery, banana, roasted coconut pieces, roasted sesame seeds, ghee and cardamom powder fried in oil. The batter made out of rice flour, jaggery and plantain is poured into a cast iron mould called *"Appa karal"* or Appakaram in which ghee is heated and fried until deep brown. It's a popular sweet dish prepared during South Indian festivals and is enjoyed by people of all age groups.Variations of this organic and spongy fried batter using jackfruit preserves instead of banana is common from the late 2000s. It is a popular snack in Kerala and are also served in the onam sadya and are also offered as prasad in some temples especially in Ganesha and Krishna temple. In Malayalam, *unni* means small and *appam* means rice cake.

Recipe:

Ingredients:

- Rice flour – 200 gms
- Suji(semolina) – 100 gms
- Ripe bananas – 2 to 3nos.
- Gur(jaggery)/sugar – 75 gms
- Coconut – ½ cup (grated)
- Elaichi(cardamom) – 4 to 5 (peel and crush)
- Baking soda – ¼ tsp
- Oil – little to fry

Method:

- Soak rice grains for 1 hour. Remove the water from the rice , spread the rice on a thick cloth so that it soaks water. Grind a fine flour of this rice.
- Mix rice flour and Suji in a big utensil. Grind coconut and sugar then put it in the utensil and mix well.
- Mash the bananas properly and put in the mixture. Also add Elaichi, followed by water and prepare a mixture thick like that of Idli. Beat the mix properly with a hand blender and keep aside for 30 minutes.
- Mix baking powder to the mixture.
- Place Appa Maker on the gas and heat it. Pour less than ¼ tsp. oil in all molds, put mixture in the molds with a spoon filling only half of it. Keep a low flame, Appam will puff up in no time and fill the mold completely. Turn over Unni Appam when its lower layer turns brown and cook till the other side turns brown.
- Take out the cooked Unni Appam in a plate and cook the other Unni Appam in this same way.
- Steaming hot Unniappam is ready, serve and eat.

XCIX
Vellum Nombu Adai

Karadaiyan Nombu is a major Tamil Nadu festival which is celebrated when Tamil month Maasi ends and month Panguni starts. Karadai is the name of a unique Nivedyam (offering for God) prepared on this day and *Nombu* means Vratham or Fasting. On this day women worship Goddess Gowri and offer her Karadaiyan Nombu Nivedyam. After Puja (prayers) women tie the sacred yellow cotton thread known as Manjal Saradu or Nombu Charadu for well – being of their husband. Married women observe it for long lives of their husband while unmarried girls observe it to get ideal person as their husband. *Vellam* means sweet, so sweet adai is prepared and served to God on banana leaves.

Recipe:

Ingredients:

- Rice Flour – 1 cup
- Jaggery – 1 cup
- Water – 1½ cup
- Coconut powder/ grated coconut – 1/4th cup
- Lobia/Black eyed peas/karamani – 1 tbsp cooked
- Cardamom powder/Elaichi – 1/4 tsp

Method:

- Pressure cook black eyes peas until soft but not mushy.
- Roast rice flour for 2 – 3 mins in medium flame. Do not roast too much. It should not turn brown. Keep it aside.

- Melt jaggery in 1½ cup of water. Do not melt it too much. Consistency should be watery.
- Add grated coconut/coconut powder and lobia/karamani/black eyed peas, cardamom powder to the jaggery water.
- Boil jaggery water, when it starts boiling, add a tsp of ghee/unsalted butter. Then reduce the flame and add rice flour slowly. Stir continuously.
- Keep the flame in medium and cook well until it leaves the sides of the pan. (Consistency should be like chappati dough). Switch off the flame and allow it to cool.
- Divide it equally, make balls, flatten it, put a hole in the center and steam the sweet adais in an idly cooker. Grease idli mould with oil & steam for 10 minutes.
- Serve with butter.

C

Zarda

Zarda is a traditional boiled sweet rice dish, native to the Indian subcontinent, with (orange) food coloring, milk and sugar, and flavoured with cardamoms, raisins, saffron, pistachios or almonds. The name Zarda comes from Persian word *'zard'* meaning 'yellow', hence named since the food coloring added to the rice gives it a yellow color. Zarda is typically served after a meal. In the Mughlai and Nizami weddings and other occasions, zarda was and still remains a popular dessert. It is also popular among the locals as *Meethe Chawal* (Sweet Rice) or *Zafrani Pulao* (as the yellow colour comes from saffron added to it. It is also called *Mittha* in Himachal Pradesh. Historically the tradition of sweet rice (Meethe Chawal) was quite common in rural Punjab & other provinces of North India where Jaggery is used to sweeten the rice (Gur Chawal). It seems that in historical time line, the Zarda is popularized in North India by Mughals. *Be it Godh Bharai ceremony, Karva Chauth, Shaadi, Raksha Bandhan, Diwali, Sankranti or Janmashtami,* this sweet treat is lovingly prepared, particularly in North Indian households and relished by all. Loaded with dry fruits and nuts, and scented with *gulab jal* or rose water and saffron, it is hard to resist. The *Ain–E–Akbari* of Abul Fazal explains the recipe of *Zard Birinj*, which constitutes rice, sugar, nuts, saffron, cinnamon, and even ginger also.

Recipe:

Ingredients:

- Long grained basmati rice – 1 cup
- Ghee butter or clarified – 1tbsps
- Water Hot – 1½ cups

- Milk warm – ½ up
- Saffron strands – ¼ tsp
- Sugar – 3/4 cup
- Nuts chopped (cashew, almonds, raisins, pistachios) – ½ cup
- Khoya or Milk solids – 1tbsps
- Cardamoms – 4 nos.
- Cloves – 6 nos.
- Cinnamon stick – ½ inch
- Nutmeg powder – ¼ tsp
- Rose water – 1 tbsp
- Saffron – a pinch

Method:

- Wash and soak the rice for 15 minutes. Soak the saffron in warm milk.
- Heat the ghee in a heavy bottomed pan, add the whole spices (cardamom, cloves and cinnamon)and when the cloves start spluttering add the chopped nuts leaving some for garnish And saute for half a minute.
- Drain the rice and add to the ghee and saute for nearly 3 minutes in low flame or till you start getting the aroma of the rice. Sautéing more than needed will break the rice grains.
- Now add the saffron soaked milk, colour if you are using, hot water, sugar, nutmeg and rose water to the rice and mix slowly.
- When it starts to boil, close the lid and cook in low flame.
- When the rice is 3/4 done, grate the khoya on it and close the lid And let the rice cook fully,
- Once done, fluff up the rice gently with a fork and serve.

CI
Summary

Sweets or Mithai form an integral part of the Indian culture, much more compared to other European and American countries. Sugar, which forms the basic ingredient for most of the sweets, has been cultivated for thousands of years in India. Even the word sugar and candy have their roots in Sanskrit, the ancient Indian language. The foremost reason for this is that there is no other country in which sweets are so varied, so numerous, or so invested with meaning as the Indian Subcontinent. India not only has a rich cultural history, its association with sweets is also millennia old. Indians were the first to refine sugar, at around 500 BC. The sugar revolution was such that by

300 BC, five different kinds of sugar were being processed in India. Indian sweets are collectively called *Mithai* which is derived from the word mitha which means sweet. There are many varieties of specific types of Indian sweets which are usually a derivative of the original recipe for the sweet. Since India unifies many cultures, traditions and cuisines thus, the cooking style and ingredients varies from one sweet to another. Indian Mithai are famous for its uniqueness, variety and irresistible taste.

Some of the common ingredients used in Indian sweets are different flours, milk, milk solids, fermented foods, root vegetables, raw and roasted seeds, seasonal fruits, fruit pastes and dry fruits. A single mithai can be of different colout taste, flavour and sizes. The method of preparation are also quite diverse using techniques like freezing for kulfi, frying for jalebi and Imarti, roasting for Mysore pak, baking for nankhatai and simple cooking for gajar ka halwa among others. Other popular sweets in the Indian subcontinent are Cham-cham, Chhenamurki, Chhena Poda, Gajrela, Gulab jamun, Rassogolla, Khaja, Kheer or payas, Laddu, Malpoa, Narkel Naru, Pathishapta, Rasgulla, Ras Malai, Sandesh, Sel Roti and Shrikhand. In fact, in India sweets have their own importance and relevance.

Whether as a form greeting, festival, celebration, religious offering, gift giving, parties or hospitality in India, sweets are an essential ingredient. It is believed that any meal is incomplete in Indian without a proper mithai or Indian sweet. Sweets signify prosperity, happiness and affection.

Especially on Indian festivals – such as Holi, Diwali, Eid, or Raksha Bhandan, the sweet shops expand to more than twice their size to keep up with the sharp increase in demand.

CII

Glossary of Indian Sweets and Desserts

1 Amras : Sweetened mango juice or pulp from Maharashtra.

2 Ada : Rice flour dough stuffed with grated coconut and jaggary. Wrapped in banana leaves and steam- from kerala.

3 Adhirasam : Small breads made from rice powder, jaggary and cardasmom, from Karnataka.

4 Anarsa : Small sweet balls made from rice flour, jaggary and nuits, from Jharkhand.

5 Ariselu : Small sweet breads made from rice flour and jaggary and is covered with poppy or white sesame seeds- from Andhra Pradesh.

6 Aval puttu : Sweet made from poha, khoya and dry fruits from Tamil Nadu.

7 Awan bangwi : Sweet pudding made from Mami rice and wrapped in Lairu leaves-from Tripura.

8 Bal mithai : Sugar, khoya and chocolate cooked together to brown in colour, and shaped and then caoated with small sugarballs (Uttarakhand)

9 Balushahi : Sweet doughnuts.

10 Barfi : Cookie shaped sweet made from khoya.

11 Basundi : It is sweet thickened milk, flavored with cardamom and nutmeg from Maharashtra.

12 Bebinca : Sweet pudding from Goa

13 Boorelu : Sweet ball or dumplings made from mixture of chana dal/ urad/mixed dal paste, jaggery, cardamom and dry nuts- from Andhra

Pradesh.

14 Cham cham : Ablong shaped sweetened fresh paneer balls coated with dry khoya from Bengal.

15 Chhanar payesh : Kheer made from Paneer. (Bengal).

16 Chhena gaja : Dry gulab jamuns made from Paneer and semolina-from Odisha.

17 Chhena jhili : Sweetened cheese patty from odisha.

18 Chhenamurki : Dry sugar dipped small paneer pieces -From Odisha.

19 Chhena poda : Burnt fresh paneer balls in charamelised sugar

20 Chikki : It is a traditional Indian sweet candy made with jaggery and peanuts or sesame seeds.

21 Danadar : Drier form of rassogulla from Bengal.

22 Dehrori : Gulgula made with rice -from Chhatisgarh.

23 Dharwad peda : Rich pedas from Karnataka

24 Dhondas : Sweet cucumber pudding from Maharashtra.

25 Dodha burfi : Rich burfi made from milk, dalia and nuts from Punjab.

26 Doodhpak : Thickened milk with nuts from Gujrat.

27 Double ka meetha : Fried bread dipped in sugar syrup of rabdi (Hyderabad)

28 Gajak : Sweet confectionb made from sesame seeds (til) or peanuts and jaggery (Uttar Pradesh)

29 Gavvalu : Maida flour shaped into shels and deep fried and then dipped in sugar syrup. (andhra Pradesh)

30 Ghari : Sweet made of puri batter, mawa, ghee and sugar.- from gujrat.

31 Ghevar : Crispy, porous deep fried sweet made from maida from Rajasthan.

32 Gujiya : Deep fried ravioli whci is stuffed with various stuffings.Perukiya -Rawa and khoya stuffed gujiya from Bihar.Somas -Besan rawa, sugar and khoya stuffed Gujiya from Tamil Nadu.Karanji- rava, coconut, sugar and dry fruits stuffed gujiya from Maharashtra.Ghughra -rava, coconut, sugar and dry fruits stuffed Gujiya from Gujrat.Nevri -coconut, sugar, poppy seeds and cardamom powder stuffed Gujiya from Goa.Kajjikaya -Coconut stuffed Gujiya from Andhra Pradesh.

33 Gulab jamun : Round fried balls of khoya and maida mixed together and dipped in sugar syrup frombengal.Ledikeni-small Gulab jamun.Pantua-small Gulab jamun, usually filled with syrup. Kalajam- black Gulab jamun.Lyancha-elongated gulab jamun.

34 Halbai : It is a pudding made with rice, jaggery and coconut. (Karnataka).

35 Halwa : It is a pudding made from semolina or maida or atta. Mahim halwa-layered semolina halwa from gujrat. Kashi halwa- ashgourd from Uttar Pradesh.

36 Imarti : Circular prezel made from urad or masoordal and dipped in sugar syrup.

37 Jalebi : Circular prezel made from mada and dipped in sugar syrup. Jhangiri-jalebi made from urad dal paste. (south india)

38 Kaju katli : Small burfi shaped cashewnut biscuits.

39 Kaju and Pista Roll : Ground pista rolled in ground cashew paste.

40 Kalakand : Sweetened milk cake.(Bihar)

41 Kanchagola : Small sweet balls nmade from fresh paneer. (bengal)

42 Khaja : Sweet puffy fritters made from maida (Bihar)

43 Khapse : Sweet north Himachali biscuit

44 Kheer : Pudding made from rice or vermicilli.

45 Kheer sagar : Marble–sized balls of chhena cheese soaked in sweetened, condensed milk. (odisha)

46 Khubani ka meetha : Sweet made from apricots (Andhra Pradesh)

47 Koat pitha : Fritter made from of rice flour, banana, powdered jaggery. (odisha)

48 Kozhukkattai : Similar to modak prepared in South india.

49 Kulfi : Sweet frozen dessert from Uttar Pradesh.

50 Laddoo : Spherical balls made with small balls of besan ot aata, coconut etc. Motichoor laddu-Ladoo made with very small beasn balls.Kobbari Kova Kajjikayalu-sweet Khoya laddu stuffed with coconut from Andhra Pradesh.Pori urundai -laddoo made with puffed rice and jaggery from Tamil Nadu.Darbesh -Laddu made with mawa , besan , sugarand ghee from Bengal.

51 Lapsi : Halwaa like sweet made from cracked wheatnuts and sugar. (Rajasthan).

52 Lassi : Sweetened semi-thick curd from Punjab.

53 Madhurjan thongba : Fried beasan balls dipped in sweetened milk-from Manipur.

54 Makhan misri : Sweet made with fresh white butter and mishri. (Gujrat).

55 Malpua : Deep fried flat cakes dipped in sugar syrup or rabdi.

56 Malai pan : Paper thin malai filled with mishri and dry fruits, shaped like pan (Uttar Pradesh).

57 Mambzha pradhaman : Sweet ripe mango puld mixed with nuts from Kerala.

58 Mawa bati : Kachoris stuffed with khoya and nuts. (Madhya Pradesh)

59 Mihindana : Very small balls of besan dipped in sugar syrup. (bengal)

60 Mishti doi : Sweetened curd from Bengal.

61 Modak : Sweet dumpling wchich is stuffed with khoya or nuts and is cone shaped (Maharashtra)

62 Mohan thaal : Soft beasn sweet with lots of ghee from Gujrat.

63 Mysore pak : Crispy and crunchy besan fudge from Karnataka.

64 Nankhatai : Sweet crunchy cookies from Uttar Pradesh.

65 Nap naang : Sweet pudding made with black sticky rice from Nagaland.

66 Narkol naru : Sweet coconut balls from Bengal.

67 Obbattu : Flour bread stuffed with sweetened chana dal (Maharashtra).

68 Palathalikalu : Sweet made with handmade rice noodles, milk, jaggery and ghee from Andhra Pradesh.

69 Panasa thonalu : Flower shaped fritter made from maida and sugar syrup dipped from Andhra Pradesh.

70 Parippu payasam : Mung dal kheer from Kerala.

71 Pateesa : Crispy, threadlike sweet made from besan. (maharashtra)

72 Patishapta : Sweetened khoya and nuts wrapped in crepes (Bengal)

73 Peda : Sweet khoya or paneer balls (Uttar Pradesh)

74 Petha : Sweet made from ash gourd (Uttar Pradesh)

75 Pitha : A kind of rice cake from Odisha.

76 Pongal : Sweetened mung dal balls from Karnataka.

77 Pootharekulu : Sweet dry fruits and nuts wrapped in paper thin rice pancakes. (andhra Pradesh)

78 Pukhlein : Sweet rice flour bread from Meghalaya.

79 Rabri : Thickened milk.

80 Rasabali : Fresh paneer patties soaked in thickened, sweetened milk. (Odisha).

81 Rasgulla : Spherical sponge like balles made from fresh paneer, dipped in sugar syrup. (Bengal)

82 Raskadam : Spherical balls of of small rasogulla covered with grated khoya from Bengal.

83 Rasmalai : Very soft paneer balls dipped in thickened sweet milk. (Bengal)

84 Rotana : Sweet cookie from Hyderabad.

85 Sael roti : Ring like sweet doughnut from Sikkim

86 Sandesh : Crumbled fresh paneer, sweetened and made into various shapes and flavours. (west bengal)

87 Shahi tukra : Fried bread coated with rabdi.

88 Shankarpali : Very small sweet puffs coated with sugar granules

89 Sheer korma : Sweet kheer made with dates, milk and sewai or vermicelli. (Mughlai).

90 Shor bhaja : Fried frsh paneer dipped in sugar syrup. (bengal)

91 Shrikhand : Sweetened fresh curd. (Maharashtra)

92 Shufta : It is a mixture of various dry fruits and spices, like (black pepper powder, dry ginger powder, cinnamon powder and cardamom powder) coated with sugar syrup. (Kashmir).

93 Sitabog : Sweetened rice and paneer small strings gasrnished witth very small gulab jamun (Nekhuti) from (Bengal).

94 Singori : Sweetened khoya wrapped in Maalu leaf (Kumaun)

95 Sohan halwa : Sweet fudge made from cornflour or maida.(Moghlai)

96 Sutarfeni : Very thin sweet rice vermicilli from Gujrat and Rajasthan

97 Thekua : Sweet fried fritter made from flour sugar or jaggary from Bihar and Jharkhand.

98 Unni appam : Sweet fritters from kerala, made with rice, jaggery, banana, roasted coconut pieces, roasted sesame seeds, ghee and cardamom powder fried in oil.

99 Vellum nombu adai : Sweet fried doughnuts from Tamil Nadu

100 Zarda : Sweetened rice , also called meethe chawal.

Know Your Author

Dr Anshumali Pandey. PhD, Author

Dr. Anshumali Pandey, is a renowned & reliable name in the field of Education, Hospitality, Tourism and Tribal Food. He is a Teacher and Chef by profession, and also an Author, a Business Auditor, and an avid culinary traveller to the Indian Sub continental hinterlands. Dr. Anshumali Pandey is a Hospitality Educator (PhD) who specialises in Higher Education, Office Administration, Pay roll, HR, Labour Laws, Audit, and Procurement & Tender Process. He is an Author with 51 Publications consisting of 36 Books.

The books written by Dr Anshumali Pandey are essentially a banquet arising from an experience of over 25 years of Professional life and have boiled down to crisp and accurate writing on his favourite subjects. Hospitality Sector champion requires to be a specialist in many fields and Dr Pandey is one of them. His knowledge is evident from the spectrum of subjects which he has chosen for his books so far, which ranges from being a specialist chef, to Master of Human resources, to Education and to love for children, and topped with Spirituality.

Books written by the Author are –

1. Theory of Indian Cookery
2. Beauty and Irony of Silvassa Tourism
3. A Short Indian Food Story

4. Be Your Own Guide to Indian Cuisine
5. Cookery Fundamentals
6. History of Indian Food (2 Editions Printed)
7. The Great Indian Story Book for Children
8. Personal Budget: Easy Work Book
9. Online Classes Log Book
10. Dictionary Making Work Book for School Children
11. The Lazy Bed
12. Hindu Dharm (हिन्दू धर्म) (In Hindi Language)
13. Where is my coffee?
14. Your First Job is Never your Last (Volume 1)
15. You are Almost There (Quick Fix Resume and Interview Hacks)
16. Working for the Enemy? - A lesson in Career Management
17. Public Speaking for the Young
18. A Date With Coffee
19. How to be The Best Hotel Front Office Employee
20. Diploma in Food Production, The complete Syllabus
21. Diploma in F&B Service, The Complete Syllabus
22. Diploma in Front Office, The Complete Syllabus
23. The Time to Speak is Now
24. Munshi Premchand (Short Stories in English)
25. The Housekeeping Department, Text Book
26. Hitchhiker's Guide to Trekking in Uttarakhand
27. Uttarakhand, A divine Land for a Reason
28. Bachhon ke liye rochak kahaniyan (बच्चों के लिए रोचक कहानियाँ) (In Hindi Language)
29. Basic Communication Skills of English
30. The Basic Office Organisation Book for Start-ups
31. Hospitality HRM
32. Hospitality Marketing
33. Bakery Ingredients and Tools
34. Human Resource Management for Indian Professionals
35. The process of LAWFULLY operating a Hospitality business in India
36. Indian Classical Sweets: History, Tradition and Recipes

Connect with me: anshumali.pandey@gmail.com
https://notionpress.com/author/337004

Author's QR Code

Please Scan the above QR Code with your Smart Phone to get online information about the Author and his Books.

9 798887 332703

Printed by Libri Plureos GmbH in Hamburg,
Germany